The Complete Air Fryer Cookbook

800 Foolproof, Quick & Easy Air Fryer Recipes for Beginners and Advanced Users

Jennifer Newman

Copyright © 2020 Jennifer Newman

All rights reserved.

No part of this guide may be reproduced in any form without permission in writing from the publisher except in the case of brief quotations embodied in critical articles or reviews.

Legal & Disclaimer

The information contained in this book and its contents is not designed to replace or take the place of any form of medical or professional advice; and is not meant to replace the need for independent medical, financial, legal, or other professional advice or services, as may be required. The content and information in this book have been provided for educational and entertainment purposes only.

The content and information contained in this book have been compiled from sources deemed reliable, and it is accurate to the best of the Author's knowledge, information and However, the Author cannot guarantee its accuracy and validity and cannot be held liable for any errors and/or omissions. Further, changes are periodically made to this book as and when needed.

You agree that by continuing to read this book, where appropriate and/or necessary, you shall consult a professional (including but not limited to your doctor, attorney, or financial advisor or such other advisor as needed) before using any of the suggested remedies, techniques, or information in this book.

Contents

Introduction..................... 8
   The Pros and Cons of the Air Fryer 8
   Tips for Using Your Air Fryer 9
   Cleaning............................ 11

Chapter 1: Breakfast Recipes........ 13
   Fried Zucchini 13
   Fried Pickles....................... 14
   Onion Rings 15
   Potatoes + Smoked Diots Sausages 16
   Poached Egg 17
   Cheeseburger 18
   Strasbourg Sausage Croissants.... 19
   Sausage Fondues 20
   Patty Mozzarella................... 21
   Strasbourg Potatoes and Sausages with Curry.......................... 22
   Treviso Chicory Sauce 23
   Sausages and Peppers 24
   Brioche Sausage................... 25
   Stuffed Potato Recipe 26

Chapter 2: *Snacks and Appetizers. 27*
   Corn with Bacon 27
   Brussels Sprouts With Bacon 28
   Frozen Croissants.................. 29

   Frozen Potato Croquettes........... 30
   Endives with Ham 31
   4 Cheese Puffs 32
   Treviso Chicory Puff Pastry 33
   Chocolate Muffins 34
   Pasticciata Pasta 35
   Shepherd's Pie 36
   Tomino With Speck................. 37
   Chickpeas for Snack 38
   Crispy Cauliflower Snacks 39
   Profiteroles....................... 40
   Feta Cheese Triangles 41
   Boudin meat 42

Chapter 3: Seafood and Fish Recipes *43*
   Grilled Sardines 43
   Spicy Squids Healthy............... 44
   Frog Thighs 46
   Exquisite Shrimp................... 48
   Shrimp Fritters.................... 49
   Cod Meatballs with Sauce........... 50
   Cod with Cherry Tomatoes and Green Olives 51
   Breaded Cod 52
   Baked Scallops with Cheese 53
   Zucchini with Tuna................. 54

Caramelized Salmon Fillet............55

Breaded Swordfish......................56

Fish and French Fries 57

Deep Fried Prawns......................58

Mussels with Pepper...................59

Scallops in Butter with Leaves.....60

Scallops in Butter........................61

Monkfish with Olives and Capers 62

Shrimp, Zucchini and Cherry Tomato Sauce 63

Spinach Crusted Salmon 64

Salmon with Pistachio Bark.........65

Salmon in Papillote With Orange 66

Salted Marinated Salmon 67

Sautéed Trout with Almonds 68

Stuffed Cuttlefish........................69

Sicilian Tuna Slices 70

Fish in Air Fryer...........................71

Rabas...72

Prawns in Ham with Red Pepper Sauce...73

Chapter 4: Poultry 74

Chopped Chicken Olive Tomato Sauce...74

Chicken Thighs in Coconut Sauce, Nuts..75

Forest Guinea Hen 76

Fried and Crispy Chicken.............77

Orange Turkey Bites 78

Chicken Thighs with Potatoes 79

Chicken Blanquette With Soy......80

Fish Sticks 81

Vegetarian Curry with Pumpkin and Chickpeas 82

Turkey Diced with Ginger, Apples and Vegetables 83

Ligurian Rabbit............................84

Frozen Chicken Nuggets..............85

Chicken with Cacciatore (Chicken Hunter).......................................86

Devil Chicken 87

Chicken with Pineapple...............88

Chicken Curry 89

Chicken with Yogurt and Mustard 90

Almond Chicken..........................91

Mushroom Chicken.....................92

Pepper Chicken...........................93

Stuffed Chicken and Baked Potatoes 94

Tandoori Chicken........................95

Crispy Chicken Fillets in Brine in Pickle Juice 96

Chapter 5: Beef, Pork, Lamb Recipes *97*

Perfect Garlic Butter Steak..........97

Crispy Pork Medallions 98

Nemos Beef with Dry Pepper Lactose Free 99
Pork and Parsni With Thai, Marinated with Honey and Soy. 100
Pork Fillet Mignon 101
Lamb with Potatoes..................102
Veal Blanquette With Peas 103
Beef Stroganoff........................104
Meatballs with Tomatoes and Peas 105
Cevapi......................................106
Milanese Chop.........................107
Lemon Chops...........................108
Amatriciana..............................109
Pork Chops with Chicory Treviso 110
Venetian Liver..........................111
Vegetable Cane........................112
Milanese Veal Legs 113
Veal, speck, and cheese paupiettes 114
Fried Pork 115
Roast Pork with Vegetables 116
Saltimbocca Roman Veal..........117
Sautéed Meat with Potatoes 118
Sautéed Pork with Peppers 119

Chapter 6: Vegan and Vegetarian Recipes *120*

Frying Potatoes........................120
Avocado Fries 121
Crispy French Fries...................122
Frying Potatoes with Butter 123
Homemade French Fries 124
Mini pepper/tomato/shallot/goat cheese tartlets..........................125
Almond Apples 126
French fries without dry............127
Bugnes Lyonnaises...................128
Green salad with roasted pepper 129
Fat Free Crispy Fries.................130
Marinated Potatoes with Chimichurri Sauce....................131
Homemade Gluten Free Spicy Chips 132
Funghetto Eggplant (Golden Neapolitan)..............................133
Fried Bananas 134
Sautéed air mushrooms and parsley......................................135
Cauliflowers au gratin 136
Peach Clafoutis 137
Zucchini thinly sliced.................138
Couscous with Vegetables 139
Rillette mushroom crusts..........140
Mediterranean Bream 141
Draniki.....................................142
Chips..143

French Fries with Paprika 144
Frozen French Fries 145
Beans in sauce 146
Spicy Potatoes 147
Frozen Potatoes 148
Potatoes (Unpeeled) And Yogurt Sauce 149
Frozen New Potatoes 150
Potatoes, Beets and Carrots 151
Frozen Onion Rings 152
Sautéed Potatoes and Pumpkin 153
Rice spaghetti with vegetables .. 154
Strapatsada 155
Chicory Strudel 156
Toast with Eggplant Caviar 157
Provencal Tomatoes 158
Potato Omelet 159
Vol Au Vent with Mushrooms ... 160
Spanish Potatoes 161
Green Salad with Roasted Pepper 162
Garlic Mushrooms 163
Roasted Potatoes with Paprika and Greek Yogurt 164
Mini peppers with Goat Cheese 165

Chapter 7: Desserts 166

Cake with cream and strawberries 166
Caramelized Pineapple and Vanilla Ice Cream 167
Apple Pie 168
Apple Rotation 169
Stuffed brioche crown 170
Fried Cream 171
Apple, cream, and hazelnut crumble 172
Fregolotta (Venetian puff pastry pie) with hazelnuts 173
Frozen Treats 174
Roscon Of Reyes (Spanish King's Cake) 175
Nut cake 176
Italian cake 177
Marble cake 178
Genoves Cake 179
Frozen Sorrentino gnocchi 180
Khachapuri (Georgian bread) 181
Sweet and Sour Onions 182
Frozen Paella 183
Spice Bread 184
Rolls 185
Small Frozen Pizzas 186
Small Slippers With Flour 187
Peas with Bacon 188
Fresh Pizza 189
Frozen Pizza 190
Poivronnade 191

Stuffed Peppers 192
Baked Apples with Cinnamon ... 193
Baked Potatoes 194
Potatoes with Small Bacon 195
Butter and bread pudding (dessert) 196
Risotto with Porcini Mushrooms 197
Speck and Cheese Roll 198
Pesto Rolled and Brie 199
Santiago's Cake 200
Cream and Pine Nuts Cake 201
Ricotta Cake 202
Ricotta Cake and Chocolate Chips 203
Amandine Pistachio Cake 204
Asparagus and Sheep Cheesecake 205

Cherry tomato and mozzarella cake 206
Tasty Chicory and Mota Cake 207
Frozen Salty Cake 208
Toad in the hole 209
Asparagus, Cheese and Speck Pie 210
Mushroom, Egg and Mozzarella Cake 211
Roasted pears 212
Gluten-Free Yogurt Cake 213
Rösti (Swiss Potatoes) 214
Thai Fish Cake with Mango Sauce 215

Conclusion 216

Introduction

Generally, frying food involves dipping it in a bowl of boiling oil. The food becomes crispy on the outside, and it usually tastes delicious, but it's also full of oil, and that much oil isn't healthy for the human body.

With air fryers, a pulsating hot air cooking system is used, which is similar to the operation of a convection oven. This leads to results where the food is crispy on the outside and tender on the inside, without the need for oil (or perhaps just one spoonful).

It almost seems too good to be true! For those who love French fries, it is a much less oily alternative that allows you to eat more often without the adverse health effects.

Again, good news! Most models allow not only frying but also cooking, baking, and roasting food. Therefore, you can use your fryer to prepare vegetables, meats, fish, and even a whole chicken, as well as cookies or cakes. In short, an air fryer can do what a conventional oven does, but only by using little to no oil.

The Pros and Cons of the Air Fryer

Pros

There are many good things about using an air fryer. Here are some of the advantages:

- Low oil use, which makes our favorite fried foods healthier
- The air fryer doesn't smell like oil, keeping the overwhelming odor out of the house when it's used
- The ability to cook an unlimited amount of food

Cons

Among the disadvantages, the cooking time of food is generally much longer with this type of fryer than in the oven or with a conventional fryer. In addition, space is more limited, which means you must cook less food at a time.

But is it really an essential accessory?

Unless you fry a lot at home, an oven also cooks most foods, not to mention potato chips are also very good. And, above all, if we limit our consumption of fries to a few occasions, we can afford to eat those cooked in a fryer!

Tips for Using Your Air Fryer

1-Attach the Control Panel

For safety reasons, if the control panel of your semi-professional fryer is not properly connected to the appliance (on both sides), your fryer will not turn on. It is important always to press the control panel down until you hear a click. In other fryers, always check that all accessories are well fixed or recessed.

2-Adding Oil

Pour oil or grease into the fryer before turning it on. Warning: without oil, the resistance may burn and damage the device.

Pour enough oil into the fryer before turning it on. The oil level must at least reach the minimum level without exceeding the maximum level. If it exceeds the prescribed amount, the oil may spill out of the fryer as soon as you dip the basket in, which could result in burns.

3-Oil Level

Take the opportunity to renew the oil. If you prefer to wait, be sure to add the same type of oil or grease. We do not recommend mixing different oils, as they can react with each other when they heat up. Each oil has its own cooking temperature and shelf life.

Important: when you add oil or grease, it is not extending the shelf life of what is already in the fryer.

If you use solid grease, melt it according to the instructions in your user manual. Keep in mind: not all fryers are suitable for using solid fats. Opt-in this case, preferably for a model equipped with a special indicator that controls the oil melting.

4-Kinds of Oil

Oil quality is an essential element. There are two types of frying oils:

Vegetable oils such as peanut oil is very suitable for frying. In addition, they are better for health because they are less abundant in bad cholesterol.

You can also prepare your fries with lard (beef fat or pork) that gives potatoes a distinctive flavor. But as shown above, not all fryers can be used with solid fat.

5-When to Change the Oil

The oil should never be dirty. Renew the oil approximately every ten uses, or sooner if it starts to get dark, smelly, or smoky. Remember that if you also use your fryer to fry sandwiches, croquettes, or donuts, you should renew the fat more often.

In the case of cold zone fryers, you will find that the oil gets dirty less quickly and can keep longer. How does a cold zone work? Under the resistance, there is an area that does not heat directly, where the temperature remains lower. Waste and crumbs are deposited at the bottom of the fryer and do not burn. Your oil stays clean for longer, and it is better for your health! Does your fryer have no cold zone? Don't panic! Filter your oil with a special paper filter, and that's it!

6-How to Make Perfect French Fries

If you put too many fries in the fryer at the same time, the oil temperature may drop too quickly, which would not guarantee optimal results. Always read the instructions on your device carefully before using it, and do not exceed the recommended amount of potato slices.

Do you want to make crispy fries on the outside and soft on the inside? Choose floury potatoes like Bintje. Later, rinse your fries thoroughly in cold water to remove as much starch as possible, then dry them at once with a clean, dry towel. Preferably cook twice. Start by previously cooking your fresh fries for 4 to 8 minutes at 150°C, and then let them cool for half an hour. Then cook them a second time at 180-190°C.

Do you use frozen fries? The first cooking is not necessary because they are already precooked. Nor is it necessary for fries to be cooked beforehand because they are very thin.

Good to know: cooking time varies depending on the type of potato used.

7-Do you use an oil-free fryer?

In principle, you should not preheat your fryer without oil, but it will take a while for the appliance to reach the desired temperature. How do you know if the fryer is ready? An indicator light comes on, or a signal is activated which indicates that the temperature has been reached and you can now adjust the preparation time.

It is not necessary to add oil. You will only need to add a tablespoon of oil if you are preparing fresh dishes such as chicken without marinade or fresh French fries. All pre-cooked foods, such as frozen fries, croquettes, and snacks, can be cooked without oil. Use peanut oil, sunflower oil, or olive oil, but never taste bad nut oil.

On some models, you should never pour the oil directly into the bowl or basket. Pour the oil over the ingredients after placing them in the pan. For models with a basket, mix the fries and oil in advance in a bowl. For best operation, do not overload the appliance and do not forget that the capacity decreases when cooking frozen food.

Cleaning

To keep the device efficient, it requires minimum maintenance. Reading the instructions is also essential, even if not all of them offer the same quality of information, advice, and warnings.

1-Anti-Odor/Anti-Grease Filters

The covers are equipped with a filter that retains steam and grease. It is metallic and permanent (fixed or removable depending on the case) and should be changed regularly: grease activated carbon anti-odor. Some fryers have a combined filter (grease and activated carbon) and another metal and permanent. The effectiveness of the filters varies depending on the device. If you retain odors during cooking, you cannot prevent them from escaping when you soak the basket in oil and when you take it out. Ideally, use the fryer in a well-ventilated room, or make sure it is equipped with an efficient hood. Logically, oil-free devices emit less odors, and hot pulsed air is recovered in the cooking chamber. Then, the odors are trapped there.

Oil must be filtered with each use to extract the crumbs that accelerate its degradation and carry risks of inflammation. In some devices, the systems facilitate the operation (filter or box). It is recommended to keep the filtered oil cold (for example, in a bottle, in the refrigerator) and change it after eight to ten uses, or as soon as it shows certain signs. If it turns brown, become viscous, smokes during heating, if foam appears, etc..

What do you do with the used oil? Do not dispose of it in the sewer or the toilet, as it contaminates while it can be recycled (biofuels). You can deposit it in a recycling center or your trash cans (in a closed bottle).

How to Make Good French Fries

When making French fries in the air fryer, golden and crispy at will, you must choose the right materials. Several varieties of potatoes are suitable: bintje, Caesar, manon or victoria. For frozen French fries, not all of them are in the same boat.

For the oil, "special frying" should be chosen. It can be sunflower, rapeseed, or olive oil for best results.

The ideal conditions for frying range is between 160 and 190°C. Under that, it is necessary to cook the fries for an extended, which makes them absorb more oil. If you cook it at higher temps,, the oil tends to decompose and release toxic compounds, such as acrylamide, in starchy foods. To prevent fries from being too greasy and limit damage, it is better to cook small amounts and cut relatively large fries (the surface area/volume ratio counts). Remove them quickly after cooking, shake the basket, and then drain on absorbent paper. At this point, they will be crispier. Baking small amounts at a time offers a second advantage in terms of color. French fries need space, since squeezing them in the basket does not suit them.

Security Questions

The precautionary statements are not useless; about fifty accidents occur every year (oil splashes, spills, fryers fire, contact burns, etc.). Do not use the device without supervision, ensure its stability, and that the cable does not drag. Use a grounded electrical outlet. Be careful when dipping frozen potato chips in oil, as water droplets can cause splashing. Gradually introduce them and remove the basket if the bath boils too much. Keep children away, and don't forget to turn your air fryer off after use. If the oil ignites, never use water! Unplug the appliance and close the lid.

Enjoy!

Chapter 1

Breakfast Recipes

Fried Zucchini

Preparation time: 15 minutes; Cooking time: 15 minutes; Serve: 2

Ingredients:

- 2 zucchinis cut into French fries
- ½ cup flour
- 2 beaten eggs
- 1 cup (250 ml) breadcrumbs
- ½ cup grated Parmesan cheese
- ¾ tsp salt, garlic, pepper to taste

Direction:

1. Preheat the air fryer to 390°F (200°C).
2. Put the flour, eggs and breadcrumbs in three different bowls.
3. Dip the fries in the flour, then the eggs and finally in the breadcrumbs. Work with about 10 French fries at a time and fry for 5 to 7 minutes or until crispy. Serve with a Caesar dressing.

Nutrition Value (Amount per serving):

- Calories 296
- Fat 15g
- Carbohydrates 31g
- Sugars 7g
- Protein 9.2g
- Cholesterol 134mg

Fried Pickles

Preparation time: 20 minutes; Cooking time: 15 minutes; Serve: 8

Ingredients:

- 32 dill pickles
- 3 large beaten eggs
- 2 tbsp dill pickle juice
- ½ cup all-purpose flour
- ½ tsp salt
- ½ tsp cayenne pepper
- ½ tsp garlic powder
- 2 cups Panko breadcrumbs
- 2 tbsp fresh dill
- Oil sprayer (optional)
- Ranch dressing

Direction:

1. Preheat the hot air fryer to 425°F (220°C).
2. Let the pickles rest on paper towels until the liquid has been absorbed (about 15 minutes).
3. In a bowl, combine the flour and salt.
4. In another bowl, whisk the eggs, pickle juice, cayenne pepper and garlic powder.
5. Combine breadcrumbs and dill in another bowl.
6. Dip each pickle in the flour on both sides and shake the excess well.
7. Dip in egg mixture, then in breadcrumbs.
8. Transfer to your fryer basket and spray with oil.
9. Fry for 7-10 minutes.
10. Serve with ranch dressing if desired.

Nutrition Value (Amount per Serving):

- Calories 32
- Fat 1.2g
- Carbohydrates 4.4g
- Sugars 0.1g
- Protein 0.8g
- Cholesterol 2.5mg

Onion Rings

Preparation time: 5 minutes; Cooking time: 16 minutes; Serve: 1

Ingredients:

- 1 large white onion
- 1 cup and ¼ flour
- 1 tsp of baking powder
- 1 beaten egg
- 1 cup milk
- ¾ cup breadcrumbs
- Seasoned salt or a mixture of paprika, salt, pepper
- 1 tbsp olive oil

Direction:

1. Spray some oil in the bottom of your fryer. If you have a temperature setting, set it to 370°F (190°C).
2. Cut the onion into rings. In a bowl, combine the flour, baking powder and add the seasoning salt (to taste).
3. Add the milk and mix well. Place the breadcrumbs on a plate.
4. Dip each slice in the dough, then in breadcrumbs and place them in the basket.
5. Add the tablespoon of oil. Cook for 8 minutes on one side, turn, and bake for another 8 minutes or until crispy.

Nutrition Value (Amount per Serving):

- Calories 580
- Fat 29g
- Carbohydrates 74g
- Sugars 19g
- Protein 8g
- Cholesterol 0mg

Potatoes + Smoked Diots Sausages

Preparation time: 10 minutes; Cooking time: 40 minutes; Serve: 2

Ingredients:

- 800 g of potatoes
- 4 Savoy smoked diots sausages
- 2 chopped onions (or 2 shallots) +10 cherry tomatoes
- 1 sprig of thyme and rosemary+1 tbsp of parsley/chopped garlic
- 3 tbsp olive oil
- 5 ml of water + white wine
- 1 tbsp of Provencal herbs + salt 5 berries
- 4 tbsp mustard tomato

Direction:

1. Peel the potatoes and cut them into cubes.
2. In the bowl of the air fryer pour the olive oil and put the onions, with the potatoes, parsley, the herbs of Provence and the salt of 5 berries. Program the fryer manually 180°C to 15 minutes.
3. When the onions and potatoes start to brown, add the sausages, cherry tomatoes, thyme, rosemary, and white wine + water. Stir with a wooden spoon.
4. Close and continue cooking. Set to 180°C - 30 minutes.
5. With a knife, check the cooking of the potatoes; otherwise, increase the cooking time by a few more minutes.
6. Remove the dish from the fryer with the tongs.
7. Enjoy this dish with mustard tomato

Nutrition Value (Amount per Serving):

- Calories 482
- Fat 37g
- Carbohydrates 24g
- Sugars 1g
- Protein 25g
- Cholesterol 57mg

Poached Egg

Preparation time: 10-20 minutes; Cooking time: 45-60 minutes; Serve: 6

Ingredients:

- 500g Eggplant
- 200g of celery
- ½ onion
- 90g olives
- 15g capers
- 40g pine nuts
- 300g ripe tomatoes
- 30g sugar
- 250g broth
- 60g vinegar
- 2 tsp olive oil
- Leave at discretion

Direction:

1. Cut the eggplant, celery and chop the onions.
2. Attach the mixing paddle to the tank.
3. Pour the oil and onion into the basket. Set the air fryer to 150^0C and brown the onion for 4 minutes.
4. Add celery, eggplant, broth and cook for another 25 minutes.
5. Season with salt and pepper. Add the pine nuts, tomato pieces, capers and olives and cook for another 15 minutes.
6. Add the sugar and vinegar at the end and cook for another 15 minutes.

Nutrition Value (Amount per Serving):

- Calories 73
- Fat 4.95g
- Carbohydrates 0.38g
- Sugars 0.38g
- Protein 6.26g
- Cholesterol 210mg

Cheeseburger

Preparation time: 0-10 minutes; Cooking time: 15-30 minutes; Serve: 4

Ingredients:

- 4 chopped steak
- 4 hamburger buns
- Salad to taste
- 1 large tomato
- Mayonnaise, ketchup, or mustard to taste
- 4 slices of cheese
- Taste oil
- Salt to taste
- Pepper to taste

Direction:

1. Season the fillets and place them in the basket. Set the air fryer 180^{0}C.
2. Cook the chopped steaks for 20 min. depending on their size turning 1-2 times during cooking.
3. Add a slice of cheese to each chopped steak and simmer for 1 minute.
4. Remove the chopped fillets from the air fryer wipe any liquid left in the basket with a cloth and heat the hamburger bread in the middle for about 1 minute.
5. Start composing the cheeseburger; spread the mayonnaise, ketchup or mustard on the bread, a salad leaf, the chopped steak with the cheese and finally the tomato slices; cover with the other slice of bread and serve.

Nutrition Value (Amount per Serving):

- Calories 343
- Fat 16.4g
- Carbohydrates 32g
- Sugars 6.7g
- Protein 17g
- Cholesterol 50mg

Strasbourg Sausage Croissants

Preparation time: 0-10 minutes, Cooking time: 15-30 minutes; Serve: 4

Ingredients:

- 1 round puff pastry roll
- 4 small sausages from Strasbourg
- Mustard to taste
- Poppy seeds to taste

Direction:

1. Unroll the puff pastry and define 16 triangles. Spread the mustard over the dough, place a small piece of Strasbourg sausage at the base of each triangle and roll until it reaches the tip. Press well to adhere.
2. Place the mini croissants in the pan, previously covered with parchment paper, well separated with the tip down; otherwise they may open during cooking.
3. Brush the mini croissants with water and sprinkle with poppy seeds.
4. Set the air fryer to 150^0C. Simmer for 13 minutes and then turn the mini croissants half a turn.
5. Simmer for another 7 min.

Nutrition Value (Amount per Serving):

- Calories 570
- Fat 40g
- Carbohydrates 32g
- Sugar 3g
- Protein 20g
- Cholesterol 275mg

Sausage Fondues

Preparation time: 10 – 20 minutes; Cooking time: 15 – 30 minutes; Serve: 4

Ingredients:

- 3 large sausages from Strasbourg
- 200g of bread dough
- Mustard (optional) to taste

Direction:

1. To prepare the poached Strasbourg sausages, start by dividing the dough into 3 equal parts (or even 6 if you want to cut the Strasbourg sausages in half).
2. Spread the dough with a rolling pin so you can completely roll up the Strasbourg sausage. Spread the mustard and place the Strasbourg sausage in the center of the rectangle, rolled up completely.
3. Moisten the bread dough to make it easier to close. Remove the excess on the sides and with a small sharp knife form transverse lines on the surface of the dough.
4. Place the Strasbourg sausages in the basket covered with parchment paper.
5. Set the temperature to 180^0C and simmer for 30 minutes.

Nutrition Value (Amount per serving):

- Calories 20
- Fat 0g
- Carbohydrates 4g
- Sugars 3g
- Protein 0.3g
- Cholesterol 0mg

Patty Mozzarella

Preparation time: 10 – 20 minutes; Cooking time: 0 – 15 minutes; Serve: 4

Ingredients:

- 12 slices of sandwich bread
- 3 eggs
- Flour to taste
- Breadcrumbs
- Leave to taste
- 12 anchovies (optional)
- 12 slices of mozzarella
- 6 slices of cooked ham

Direction:

1. Take the slices of bread and remove the crust. Cut 2 rectangles on each slice. Fill each rectangle with a slice of mozzarella, ½ slice of ham and 1 anchovy.
2. Then close everything with a slice of bread.
3. Put the eggs in a bowl, in another the flour and in a third the breadcrumbs.
4. Take the sandwiches and pass them on both sides first in the flour, then in the egg and finally in the breadcrumbs, welding well to prevent the mozzarella from coming out during cooking.
5. If you prefer, you can iron the sandwiches in the egg and in the breadcrumbs.
6. Grease the basket and preheat it for 1 minute at 150^0C.
7. Add mozzarella and continue cooking for 8 minutes, turning halfway through cooking.

Nutrition Value (Amount per Serving):

- Calories 290
- Fat 15 g
- Carbohydrates 24 g
- Sugars 2g
- Protein 11 g
- Cholesterol 35 mg

Strasbourg Potatoes and Sausages with Curry

Preparation time: 10-20 minutes; Cooking time: 15-30 minutes; Serve: 6

Ingredients:

- 750 g of fresh potatoes
- 3 Strasbourg sausages
- 2 small spoons of curry
- Salt to taste

Direction:

1. Peel the potatoes and cut them into cubes of approximately 1 cm per side. Put the Perl apples to soak in water, drain them and dry them well with a paper towel.
2. After spraying the air fryer with cooking spray, pour potatoes, salt.
3. Set the temperature to 150^{0}C and simmer the potatoes for 20 minutes.
4. Add the Strasbourg sausages cut into small pieces, curry, and cook for another 10 minutes.

Nutrition Value (Amount per Serving):

- Calories 418.5
- Fat 17.6 g
- Carbohydrate 42.1 g
- Sugars 2.1 g
- Protein 18.0 g
- Cholesterol 44.5 mg

Treviso Chicory Sauce

Preparation time: 10-20 minutes, Cooking time: 15-30 minutes; Serve: 6

Ingredients:

- 400g of Treviso chicory
- 1 leek
- ½ red wine
- Salt to taste

Direction:

1. Chop the leek and place it in the basket previously greased.
2. Cook for 3 minutes at 160^0C.
3. Add the previously cleaned chicory cut into large pieces, pour the red wine and salt. Cook for an added 12 minutes. Ideal for filling pancakes, lasagna, savory cakes, etc.

Nutrition Value (Amount per Serving):

- Calories 20
- Fat 0g
- Carbohydrates 4g
- Protein 1g

Sausages and Peppers

Preparation time: 0-10 minutes, Cooking time: 15-30 minutes; Serve: 4

Ingredients:

- 4 sausages
- 2 peppers

Direction:

1. Pour the sausages and peppers cut into pieces in the basket.
2. Cook for 20 minutes at 150^0C.

Nutrition Value (Amount per Serving):

- Calories 339
- Sugars 3g
- Fat 27g
- Protein 17g
- Carbohydrates 5.8g
- Cholesterol 84mg

Brioche Sausage

Preparation time: 0 – 10 minutes, Cooking time: 0 – 15 minutes; Serve: 4

Ingredients:

- 2 sausages
- 2 bread sticks

Direction:

1. Remove the crumb from the bread to obtain a hollow cylinder (make pieces of about 10 cm, otherwise it will be difficult to work them).
2. Place the sausage in half the bread, then make slices about 2 cm thick.
3. Place the slices at the bottom of the basket (6 per batch).
4. Set the temperature to 160^0C.
5. Cook for 10 minutes, turning the crispy rolls on themselves after 5/6 minutes.
6. Serve while it is still hot.

Nutrition Value (Amount per Serving):

- Calories 546
- Carbohydrates 37g
- Fat 35g
- Sugars 6g
- Protein 20g
- Cholesterol 0mg

Stuffed Potato Recipe

Preparation time: 20 minutes; Cooking time: 14 minutes; Serve: 4

Ingredients:

- 150g Potatoes
- Ham
- Cheese
- Olive oil
- Salt
- Garlic powder

Direction:

1. Cut your potato into strips but don't get to the end.
2. Paint your potato with a little oil so it doesn't burn.
3. Add salt and pepper.
4. Put the potato 35 minutes at 180°C without preheating.
5. Fill each cut with ham and cheese to taste.
6. Put the potato back 10 minutes more at 180°C.

Nutrition Value (Amount per Serving):

- Calories 379.6
- Fat 17.6 g
- Carbohydrate 40.7 g
- Sugars 4.0 g
- Protein 14.0 g
- Cholesterol 25.4 mg

Chapter 2

Snacks and Appetizers

Corn with Bacon

Preparation time: 0-10; Cooking time: 15-30; Serve: 4

Ingredients:

- 4 Precooked corn on the cob
- 8 Sliced Bacon

Direction:

1. Roll up the corn cobs with 2 slices of bacon each.
2. Place the corn cobs inside, close the lid.
3. Set the air fryer to 180^0C and Cook the corn on the cob for 15 minutes.

Nutrition Value (Amount per Serving):

- Calories 90
- Sugars 0g
- Fat 7g
- Protein 5g
- Carbohydrate 0g
- Cholesterol 15mg

Brussels Sprouts With Bacon

Preparation time: 0-10 minutes; Cooking time: 15-30 minutes; Serve: 6

Ingredients:

- 350g Brussels sprouts
- 20g butter
- 100g of bacon

Direction:

1. Clean the Brussels sprouts by removing the outer leaves and the base. Steam for about 20 min.
2. Place the bacon and butter in the bowl. Set the air fryer to 150^0C and brown for 5 min.
3. Add the puff pastry, salt, and simmer for 10 min. additional, depending on the size of the cabbage.

Nutrition Value (Amount per Serving):

- Calories 287
- Sugars 3.8g
- Fat 18g
- Protein 18g
- Carbohydrates 16g
- Cholesterol 36mg

Frozen Croissants

Cooking time: 30-45 minutes; Serve: 4

Ingredients:

- 4 pieces of frozen croissants

Direction:

1. Preheat the air fryer at 150^0C for 5 minutes.
2. Place the croissants in the basket.
3. Cook everything for 35 minutes. Turn it to 180°C (using parchment paper) after about 25 min.

Nutrition Value (Amount per Serving):

- Calories 201
- Carbohydrates 19g
- Fat 11g
- Sugars 2g
- Protein 4g
- Cholesterol 0mg

Frozen Potato Croquettes

Cooking time: 15-30 minutes; Serve: 6

Ingredients:

- 750 g frozen potato croquette
- Fine salt to taste

Direction:

1. Preheat the air fryer at 180^0C for 5 minutes.
2. Pour the potatoes in the basket. Cook everything for 24 minutes.
3. Salt and serve.

Nutrition Value (Amount per Serving):

- Calories 54
- Carbohydrates 6g
- Fat 2g
- Sugars 0g
- Protein 0.5g
- Cholesterol 0mg

Endives with Ham

Preparation time: 20-30 minutes; Cooking time: 15-30 minutes; Serve: 6

Ingredients:

- 6 endives
- 500 ml of bechamel
- 6 slices of cooked ham
- 100g grated cheese

Direction:

1. Clean the Belgian chicory and steam for 15 min. Let them cool.
2. Separately, prepare ½ liter of bechamel and, as soon as it is ready, pour half the grated cheese and mix.
3. Pour the béchamel sauce in the bottom of the tank, roll each endive with a slice of ham, and place them too. Cover everything with the remaining bechamel and sprinkle with grated cheese.
4. Set the temperature to 150^0C and cook for 15 minutes depending on the degree of gold desired.

Nutrition Value (Amount per Serving):

- Calories 106
- Fat 5.77 g
- Carbohydrates 5.69 g
- Sugars 2.67 g
- Proteins 6.2 g
- Cholesterol 0mg

4 Cheese Puffs

Preparation time: 10-20 minutes; Cooking time: 15-30 minutes; Serve: 4

Ingredients:

- 1 rectangular puff pastry
- 250 g cheese mix
- Poppy seeds

Direction:

1. Unroll the puff pastry roll and cut it into 4 equal parts. Fill each rectangle with the cheeses cut into pieces and close the dough, welding the edges so that it does not open during cooking. This is the area of the puff pastry with water and sprinkle with poppy seeds.
2. Place 2 or 4 puff pastry (depending on its size) on the baking paper inside the basket.
3. Set the temperature to 150^0C.
4. Cook for 20 minutes or until desired browning is achieved.

Nutrition Value (Amount per Serving):

- Calories 140
- Fat 6g
- Carbohydrates 19g
- Sugars 1g
- Protein 2g
- Cholesterol 160mg

Treviso Chicory Puff Pastry

Preparation time: 0-10 minutes, Cooking time: 15-30 minutes; Serve: 4

Ingredients:

- 1 stalk of Treviso chicory
- 1 roll of puff pastry
- Grated cheese to taste
- Salt to taste
- 1 tsp olive oil

Direction:

1. Cut the chicory of Treviso in 4 parts, wash carefully and dry.
2. Unwind the puff pastry on a work surface and cut it into small wide strips of approximately 1 cm. Roll the chicory in a spiral with the puff pastry, and more particularly outside, which would otherwise dry during cooking.
3. Cover the bottom of the basket with parchment paper. Place the chicory inside, sprinkle with grated cheese and salt.
4. Set the temperature to 180^0C.
5. Simmer for 18 minutes; before serving, pour a drizzle of olive oil in each puff pastry.

Nutrition Value (Amount per Serving):

- Calories 170
- Carbohydrates 11g
- Fat 13g
- Sugars 0g
- Protein 2g
- Cholesterol 35 mg

Chocolate Muffins

Preparation time: 10-20 minutes; Cooking time: 15-30 minutes; Serve: 10

Ingredients:

- 300g of flour 00:
- 300g of sugar
- 150g of butter
- 70g bitter cocoa powder
- 6g baking powder
- 180 ml of whole fresh milk
- 1g of salt
- Eggs
- 2g of baking soda
- 100g dark chocolate
- 1 vanilla pod

Direction:

1. In a food processor, beat the butter of the ointment with the sugar and then combine the seeds of a vanilla bean.

2. When the mixture is clear and foamy enough, add the eggs at room temperature, one at a time. Work all the ingredients for a few minutes and then add the flour, bitter cocoa, yeast, baking soda and salt (all sifted), alternating with milk at room temperature.

3. Finally, combine the dark chocolate chips

4. Fill the molds with the mixture and place them inside the air fryer (7 to 8 lots) previously preheated at 180°C.

5. Cook for about 25 minutes. In the end let cool. You can, at discretion, sprinkle with icing sugar.

Nutrition Value (Amount per Serving):

- Calories
- Fat 38g
- Carbohydrates 79.2g
- Sugars 47.9g
- Protein 9.9g
- Cholesterol 125mg

Pasticciata Pasta

Preparation time: 20 – 30 minutes, Cooking time: 0 – 15 minutes; Serve: 6

Ingredients:

- 300g of macaroni
- 500 ml of bechamel
- 350 g minced meat
- 100 g cooked ham
- 30 g grated cheese

Direction:

1. Prepare the béchamel and cook the macaroni, making sure that they are firm when biting, once cooked, season them with separately cooked ground beef and ¾ of bechamel.
2. Pour the béchamel in the bowl, add half of the seasoned dough, cut the ham into small pieces, and pour the remaining dough. Sprinkle with grated cheese.
3. Set the air fryer to 150^0C cook for about 10 min. or until the desired gold is obtained.

Nutrition Value (Amount per Serving):

- Calories 576
- Carbohydrates 58g
- Fat 25g
- Sugars 0g
- Protein 26g
- Cholesterol 0mg

Shepherd's Pie

Preparation time: 10-20 minutes; Cooking time: more than 60 minutes; Serve: 8

Ingredients:

- 700 g of minced meat
- 350 g of tomato coulis
- 1 carrot
- 1 celery stalk
- 1 shallot
- Salt to taste
- Black pepper to taste
- 300 g of frozen peas

Ingredients for the cover:

- 1 kg of potatoes
- 200 g of milk
- 80 g butter
- 2 egg yolks
- Nutmeg to taste

Direction:

1. Divide the carrots, celery and chopped onions and then spray the basket. Brown for 5 minutes at 160^0C.
2. Add the minced meat and cook for 5 minutes (during this time, using a wooden spoon, possibly separate the pieces of meat that can form). Add the tomato, salt and pepper coulis and cook for 45 minutes, mixing 3 to 4 times during cooking.
3. Finally, add the frozen peas and cook for another 10 to 15 minutes until the peas are tender.
4. Remove the blade (be careful that it is hot!) And spread the sauce with a tablespoon. Prepare the mash (according to the indicated doses) and then, using a bag of fluted puff pastry, make a lot of mash in the meat.
5. Brown everything for another 10 to 15 minutes. Let stand for 10 minutes before serving.

Nutrition Value (Amount per Serving):

- Calories 272
- Fat 8.21g
- Carbohydrate 34.46g
- Sugars 3.26g
- Protein 15.55g
- Cholesterol 34mg

Tomino With Speck

Preparation time: 0 – 10 minutes, Cooking time: 0 – 15 minutes; Serve: 4

Ingredients:

- 4 tominos
- 8 speck slices

Direction:

1. Wrap the tominos with two slices of speck each, crossing them.
2. Cook the tominos for 5 minutes at 150^0C.
3. Turn them on and cook for another 3 minutes.

Nutrition Value (Amount per Serving):

- Calories 361
- Carbohydrates 2g
- Fat 30g
- Sugars 0g
- Protein 20g
- Cholesterol 0mg

Chickpeas for Snack

Preparation time: 10 minutes; Cooking time: 25 minutes; Serve: 6

Ingredients:

- 1 can (15 ounces) unsalted chickpeas, washed and drained
- Cooking spray oil
- ½ tsp garlic powder
- ½ tsp thyme powder
- ½ tsp coarsely ground black pepper
- 1/8 tsp red pepper or to taste

Direction:

1. Pour the chickpeas in a medium bowl. Dry them with a paper towel. Spray the chickpeas with the cooking spray oil for 2 seconds and stir to cover all the chickpeas. Pour them into the fryer basket.

2. In a small bowl, mix the garlic powder, the thyme powder, the pepper, and the red pepper; Set the bowl aside.

3. Adjust the temperature to 375°F and fry in air for 10 to 15 minutes or until the chickpeas are golden and crispy. Shake the fryer basket every 5 minutes. Halfway through the cooking time, sprinkle the chickpeas with cooking spray oil for 1 second.

4. Place the hot chickpeas in a bowl. Mix them with the seasoning immediately. Serve them warm or let the crispy chickpeas cool and dry completely, then store them in an airtight container at room temperature.

Nutrition Value (Amount per Serving):

- Calories 80
- Fat 1.5 g
- Carbohydrates 13 g
- Fiber 4g
- Sugar 2g
- Protein 4g

Crispy Cauliflower Snacks

Preparation time: 5 minutes; Cooking time: 10 minutes; Serve: 4

Ingredients:

- 3 cups small cauliflower florets
- 1 tbsp olive oil
- ¼ tsp garlic powder
- 3 tbsp whole grain breadcrumbs
- 2 tbsp wing sauce

Direction:

1. In a medium bowl, mix the cauliflower florets with olive oil, garlic powder and breadcrumbs.
2. Place the cauliflower in the fryer basket. Set the temperature to 400°F and fry in air for 3 to 4 minutes. Shake the basket. Fry in air for 2 to 4 minutes or until the cauliflower is tender and the edges are crispy.
3. Transfer the cauliflower to a bowl and mix with the wing sauce. Serve warm.

Nutrition Value (Amount per Serving):

- Calories 70
- Fat 4g
- Carbohydrates 9g
- Fiber 2g
- Sugars 3g
- Protein 4g

Profiteroles

Preparation time: 25 minutes; Cooking time 25 minutes; Serve: 10

Ingredients:

- 100 g flour
- 100 g of butter
- 200 g of water
- 200 g large eggs
- ¼ tsp of salt

Filling:

- 1 package vanilla pudding instant mix
- 240 ml milk
- 1 cup thick cream

Direction:

1. Mix the contents of the instant vanilla pudding mixture with 240 ml of cold milk in a bowl. Beat these ingredients with the double accessory to mix for 2 minutes. Cover and refrigerate to sit for at least 5 minutes.

2. Beat the thick cream with the whisk or the double mixing accessory. Add the whipped cream to the pudding mixture. Cover and refrigerate.

3. In a large pot, place water and butter until they boil. Over medium heat, stir so that it boils. Over medium heat, add flour and salt. Stir vigorously until the dough forms a ball in the center of the pan. Transfer the dough to a large mixing bowl and let stand for 5 minutes. With the double accessory to mix, beat the eggs one by one and mix well. Pour per tablespoon, 5 cm/2 apart, on an ungreased baking sheet.

4. Bake for 25 minutes at 218°C (425°F) until it reaches a golden-brown hue. The centers must be dry.

5. When the profiteroles are cold, you can split them and fill them with the pudding mix or use a pastry bag to introduce the pudding into the profiteroles.

Nutrition Value (Amount per Serving):

- Calories 170
- Fat 13g
- Carbohydrates 11g
- Fiber 0g
- Sugars 6g
- Protein 2g

Feta Cheese Triangles

Preparation time: 20 minutes; Cooking time: 9 minutes; Serve: 3

Ingredients:

- 1 egg yolk
- 100 g feta cheese
- 2 tbsp chopped parsley
- 1 chive in thin rings
- Freshly ground black pepper
- 5 sheets of frozen phyllo dough

Direction:

1. Beat the egg yolk in a bowl and mix it with feta cheese, parsley, and chives; Season with pepper to taste.
2. Cut each sheet of phyllo dough into three strips.
3. Take a teaspoon full of the feta mixture and place it on the inside of a strip of pasta.
4. Fold the tip of the dough over the filling to form a triangle, and then fold the zigzag tip until the filling is wrapped in a dough triangle.
5. Fill the other strips of pasta with feta in the same way. Preheat the air fryer to 200°C. Spread the triangles with a little oil and place five of them in the basket. Insert the basket in the air fryer and set the timer to 3 minutes.
6. Bake the feta triangles until golden brown. Bake the rest of the triangles in the same way. Serve the triangles on a tray.

Nutrition Value (Amount per Serving):

- Calories 89
- Fat 3.6g
- Carbohydrates 11.7g
- Sugar 0.3g
- Protein 3g

Boudin meat

Preparation time: 10 minutes; Cooking time: 25 minutes; Serve: 4

Ingredients:

- 400 g lean minced beef
- 1 lightly beaten egg
- 3 tbsp breadcrumbs
- 50 g of salami or chorizo well chopped
- 1 small onion, well chopped
- 1 tbsp fresh thyme
- Freshly ground pepper
- 2 mushrooms in thick slices
- 1 tbsp olive oil

Direction:

1. Preheat the air fryer to 200°C.
2. Mix the minced meat in a bowl with the egg, breadcrumbs, salami, onion, thyme, 1 teaspoon of salt and a generous amount of pepper. Knead it all right.
3. Pass the minced meat to the tray or platter and smooth the top. Place the mushrooms by pressing a little and cover the top with olive oil.
4. Place the tray or dish in the basket and insert it into the air fryer. Set the timer to 25 minutes and roast the meat pudding until it has a nice toasted color and is well done.
5. Let the pudding stand at least 10 minutes before serving. Then cut it into wedges. It is delicious with chips and salad.

Nutrition Value (Amount per Serving):

- Calories 200
- Carbohydrates 10g
- Fat 15g
- Sugars 0g
- Protein 5g
- Cholesterol 0mg

Chapter 3

Seafood and Fish recipes

Grilled Sardines

Preparation time: 5 minutes; Cooking time: 21 minutes; Serve: 2

Ingredients:

- 5 sardines
- Herbs of Provence

Direction:

1. Preheat the air fryer to 160^0C.
2. Spray the basket and place your sardines in the basket of your fryer.
3. Set the timer for 14 minutes. After 7 minutes, remember to turn the sardines so that they are roasted on both sides.

Nutrition Value (Amount per Serving):

- Calories 189g
- Sugars 0g
- Fat 10g
- Protein 22g
- Carbohydrates 0g
- Cholesterol 128mg

Spicy Squids Healthy

Preparation time: 10 minutes; Cooking time: About fifteen minutes; Serve: 2

Ingredients:

- 300 g of squid slices, about 20
- ½ cup milk or vegetable drink (me, almond)
- 2 cloves garlic, pressed
- 2 pinches of salt
- Curry lining
- 4g breadcrumbs
- 4g cornmeal (semolina no. 400, texture close to polenta)
- 4 g freshly grated Parmesan cheese
- ¼ tsp Curry powder Madras
- ¼ tsp turmeric
- 1/8 tsp of garam masala
- Salt and pepper to taste
- 2 tbsp olive oil

Direction:

1. Rinse the squids in cold water, put them in a bowl and cover them with milk. Add salt and garlic and mix well. Cover the bowl and let it rest in the fridge for 1 hour, then let it cool 30 minutes before cooking.
2. Clean the squid with paper towels without insisting. In a bowl, combine the ingredients of the coating, except the oil. Roll the squid one by one in the dry pie to cover them well. Place them on a plate and lightly apply a little oil on each washer.
3. Heat the air fryer to 400°F. As soon as it is cooked, place the squid in the fryer basket. Cook for 5 minutes, remove the basket, and shake well. Repeat these operations two or three times more, always counting 5 minutes of cooking and stirring the basket. I left yesterday 15 minutes in total; the squid would have preferred 5 more.
4. Accompanied here of fried pak-choy, rice and a small sauce made with mayonnaise and yogurt.

Nutrition Value (Amount per Serving):

- Calories 264
- Carbohydrates 18g
- Fat 9g

- Protein 20g
- Sugars 11g
- Cholesterol 0mg

Frog Thighs

Preparation time: 15 minutes; Cooking time: 20 minutes; Serve: 2

Ingredients:

- 1 454 g bag of frog legs, thawed and dried
- 3 tsp flour
- 1 beaten egg
- 1 tbsp of neutral oil, such as grape seed
- Clementine marinade
- The juice of 2 Clementine
- ½ orange zest
- 2 tbsp neutral oil
- 1 tsp rice vinegar
- 1 tsp tamari or soy sauce, reduced in salt
- 1 tsp fish sauce
- Crunchy coating
- ½ cup panko
- ½ orange zest
- 3 tsp Parmesan
- 2 tbsp unsweetened coconut flakes

Direction:

1. On a plate that can contain frog legs, prepare the marinade by combining all the ingredients. Using a fork for fondue, pierce the skin of the thighs in several places before macerating in the refrigerator, the dish covered with a plastic wrap, between 6 and 8 hours or overnight, and not just 2 hours.

2. 30 minutes before cooking, remove the thighs from the refrigerator. Prepare three deep plates, one with the flour, one second with the beaten egg, the last with the crunchy layer.

3. Start by flouring a thigh, soak it in the beaten egg and then roll it in the crunchy layer before placing it on a plate. Do the same with the other thighs. With a pastry brush, finish with a light layer of oil on each of its two sides.

4. Heat the air fryer to 400°F, place all thighs in the basket and cook for 5 minutes. Remove the basket, shake it, and replace it for another 3 minutes, remove it and shake it, then another 2 minutes.

5. Served here with grilled bok-choy mini petals and basmati rice.

Nutrition Value (Amount per Serving):

- Calories 75
- Carbohydrates 0g
- Fat 0.3g

- Protein 16.4g
- Sugars 0g
- Cholesterol 50mg

Exquisite Shrimp

Preparation time: 10 minutes; Cooking time: 7 minutes; Serve: 2

Ingredients:

- 20 raw shrimp 31-40, thawed and well dried
- 3 tsp flour
- 1 egg
- 2 tbsp of neutral oil, grapeseed or other
- Crunchy coating
- 2/3 cup panko (uncooked Japanese breadcrumbs)
- 3 tsp freshly grated Parmesan cheese
- 2 tbsp unsweetened coconut flakes
- ½ tsp turmeric
- ½ tsp curry powder

Direction:

1. In a small bowl, put the flour. In another small bowl, beat the egg. In a third larger bowl, for example, a deep dish, combine the ingredients for the crispy coating and mix well.
2. Press a shrimp in the flour on both sides, soak it in the egg, then press it again on both sides, this time in the crunchy layer.
3. Place on a plate and do the same with all shrimp to cook.
4. With a brush, lightly brush all shrimp with oil, turn them over and brush the other side.
5. Place them one by one in the basket of the preheated air fryer at 180^0C and replace them in the appliance. Wait 7 minutes, remove the basket, and place it on a heat resistant surface. Using a pair of silicone tweezers, remove the shrimp and serve.

Nutrition Value (Amount per Serving):

- Calories 6
- Fat 0.1g
- Carbohydrate 0.05g
- Protein 1.22g
- Sugars 0g
- Cholesterol 9mg

Shrimp Fritters

Preparation time: about 15 minutes; Cooking time: 10 to 15 minutes; Serve: 4

Ingredients:

- 100g of flour
- 50g of cornstarch
- 50 ml of milk (to adapt to not have a paste too liquid)
- 1 sachet of baking powder
- 2 eggs
- 1 tbsp peanut or sunflower oil
- Salt and pepper
- Spices at your convenience
- 20 to 25 shrimp

Direction:

1. In a bowl, mix the flour, cornstarch, and baking powder.
2. Create a well in the middle and pour the eggs you have already beaten. Add salt, pepper, and spices if you choose to add them.
3. Mix everything while beating the dough so that it is very uniform and then let stand for 1:30.
4. Peel your shrimp while keeping your tail.
5. Once the dough is rested, dip each shrimp in it to cover it perfectly.
6. Cook:
7. Place the donuts in the fryer without oil for 10 to 15 minutes at 150^0C. Check the cooking and take them out as soon as the dough is golden brown.

Nutrition Value (Amount per Serving):

- Calories 137
- Carbohydrates 8g
- Fat 9g
- Protein 4g
- Sugars 1g
- Cholesterol 32mg

Cod Meatballs with Sauce

Preparation time: 10 – 20; Cooking time: 15 - 30, 6 people.

Ingredients:

- 350g cod heart
- 50g breadcrumbs
- 1 bunch of parsley
- Thyme to taste
- 1 egg
- 1 clove garlic
- 40g grated cheese
- Salt, pepper, flour to taste
- Tartar sauce to taste

Direction:

1. To prepare the meatballs, start by mixing the breadcrumbs in a food processor. Then add the fish, thyme, chopped parsley, garlic, grated cheese, eggs and add (at discretion) salt and pepper.
2. Collect the preparation and form balls by hand. Flour each dough ball and roll them into a skewer (3 balls of dough per skewer).
3. Place the skewers in the basket of the air fryer. Close to cook at 180^0C for 10 minutes by turning the skewers while cooking.
4. Cook for an additional 10 minutes.
5. Serve with tartar sauce.

Nutrition Value (Amount per Serving):

- Calories 40
- Fat 2.9 g
- Carbohydrates 0.9 g
- Sugars 0.5 g
- Protein 2.7 g
- Cholesterol 15 mg

Cod with Cherry Tomatoes and Green Olives

Preparation time: 10-20; Cooking time: 30-45; Serve: 4

Ingredients:

- 400g cod
- 250 g cherry tomatoes
- 350 g of potatoes in pieces
- 100 g of green olives
- Salt to taste
- 1 clove garlic
- 1 tsp olive oil

Direction:

1. Put the cod in the center. Add small tomatoes, cut in half, olives, chopped potatoes, garlic clove, oil, and salt.
2. Set the air fryer to 150^0C and Cook everything for 25 min. and then mix the vegetables with a wooden spoon to homogenize the cooking.
3. Cook for an additional 15 minutes; the cooking time varies according to the size at which you will cut the potatoes

Nutrition Value (Amount per Serving):

- Calories 226.0
- Fat 2.7 g
- Carbohydrate 6.9 g
- Sugars 2.4 g
- Protein 40.6 g
- Cholesterol 99.1 mg

Breaded Cod

Preparation time: 10-20; Cooking time: 15-30; Serve: 4

Ingredient:

- 400g cod
- 2 eggs
- Flour at discretion
- Unlimited Breadcrumbs
- Parsley at discretion
- Chives at discretion
- Leave at discretion
- 1 tsp olive oil

Direction:

1. Clean the cod and cut it into pieces according to the desired size.
2. Beat the eggs on a first plate with a pinch of salt; in a second dish put the flour and in a third mix the breadcrumbs, parsley, and chives.
3. Pour the oil into the basket of the air fryer and distribute it throughout the surface.
4. Pass each slice of cod first in the flour, then in the beaten egg and finally in the breadcrumbs; arrange the slices in the tank.
5. Set the air fryer to 150^0C and cook for 10 minutes.
6. Turn the fish over and cook for another 6 minutes. Ideal accompanied by a sauce (yogurt, mayonnaise, etc.)

Nutrition Value (Amount per Serving):

- Calories 156
- Fat 2.3g
- Carbohydrates 16.4g
- Sugars 1.9g
- Protein 16.6g
- Cholesterol 0mg

Baked Scallops with Cheese

Preparation time: 10 – 20; Cooking time: 15 – 30; Serve: 4

Ingredients:

- 4 scallops
- 40 g of breadcrumbs: 40 g
- 25 g grated cheese
- 1 tbsp parsley
- 1 tsp oil
- Salt to taste
- 1 clove of garlic (optional)

Direction:

1. Combine breadcrumbs, parsley, cheese, garlic, and salt in a bowl.
2. Place the scallops in the tank and cover them with the previously made filling, covered with a drizzle of olive oil.
3. Preheat the air fryer to 150^0C for 5 minutes.
4. Cook for 17 min. or until the desired cooking is obtained; before serving, add a drizzle of olive oil.

Nutrition Value (Amount per Serving):

- Calories 218.2
- Fat 14.0 g
- Carbohydrate 12.5 g
- Sugars 1.3 g
- Protein 10.0 g
- Cholesterol 35.0 mg

Zucchini with Tuna

Preparation time: 10 – 20; Cooking time: 15 – 30; Serve: 2

Ingredients:

- 4 medium zucchini
- 120g of tuna in oil (canned) drained
- 30g grated cheese
- 1 tsp pine nuts
- Salt, pepper to taste

Direction:

1. Cut the zucchini in half lengthwise and empty it with a small spoon (set aside the pulp that will be used for filling); place them in the basket.
2. In a food processor, put the zucchini pulp, drained tuna, pine nuts and grated cheese. Mix everything until you get a homogeneous and dense mixture.
3. Fill the zucchini. Set the air fryer to 180^0C.
4. Simmer for 20 min. depending on the size of the zucchini. Let cool before serving

Nutrition Value (Amount per Serving):

- Calories 389
- Carbohydrates 10g
- Fat 29g
- Sugars 5g
- Protein 23g
- Cholesterol 40mg

Caramelized Salmon Fillet

Preparation time: 0-10; Cooking time: 15-30; Serve: 4

Ingredients:

- 2 salmon fillets
- 60g cane sugar
- 4 tbsp soy sauce
- 50g sesame seeds
- Unlimited Ginger

Direction:

1. Preheat the air fryer at 180^0C for 5 minutes.
2. Put the sugar and soy sauce in the basket.
3. Cook everything for 5 minutes.
4. In the meantime, wash the fish well, pass it through sesame to cover it completely and place it inside the tank and add the fresh ginger.
5. Cook for 12 minutes.
6. Turn the fish over and finish cooking for another 8 minutes.

Nutrition Value (Amount per Serving):

- Calories 569
- Fat 14.9 g
- Carbohydrates 40 g
- Sugars 27.6 g
- Protein 66.9 g
- Cholesterol 165.3 mg

Breaded Swordfish

Preparation time: 10-20; Cooking time: 15-30; Serve:

Ingredients:

- 500g swordfish ranches:
- Breadcrumbs to taste
- 1 tsp peanut oil
- 1 tsp olive oil
- ½ lemon juice:
- Salt to taste
- Pepper to taste
- Parsley to taste

Direction:

1. Clean and rinse the fish; grease each slice and pass it in lightly salted breadcrumbs to cover it completely.
2. Preheat the air fryer at 160^0C for 5 minutes.
3. Place the breaded fish in the basket. Cook the fish for 10 minutes.
4. Turn the fish over and cook for another 8 minutes.
5. Meanwhile, prepare the marinade with olive oil, lemon juice, salt, pepper and chopped parsley; Mix with a fork.
6. Once ready, place the fish slices on the plate and pour 1 to 2 tablespoons of marinade.

Nutrition Value (Amount per Serving):

- Calories 67
- Fat 3.79g
- Carbohydrates 2.23g
- Sugars 0.22g
- Protein 5.67g
- Cholesterol 16mg

Fish and French Fries

Preparation time: 10-20; Cooking time: 30-45; Serve: 2

Ingredients:

- 400g cod fillets
- 2 eggs
- Breadcrumbs
- Leave to taste
- Flour to taste
- 1 tsp peanut oil
- 500g of frozen French fries

Direction:

1. Clean the fish and cut it into rectangles of about 8 to 10 cm by 4 cm. Pass each slice first in the flour, then in the egg (beaten with salt) and finally in the breadcrumbs; in the end, pass them again in the egg and in the breadcrumbs to obtain a double pie.
2. Grease the basket and preheat the air fryer at 160^0C for 5 minutes.
3. Cook the fish for 10 minutes.
4. Turn the fish over and cook for another 5 minutes.
5. At the end, clean the tank and insert the mixing paddle inside and then the potatoes.
6. Cook the French fries for 20 minutes or according to the desired degree of cooking.
7. At the end of cooking, remove the preparation paddle, place the previously cooked fish in the fries and reheat it for approximately 2 to 3 minutes.

Nutrition Value (Amount per Serving):

- Calories 79
- Fat 3g
- Carbohydrates 12.2g
- Sugars 0g
- Protein 0.8g
- Cholesterol 167mg

Deep Fried Prawns

Preparation time: 10 – 20; Cooking time: 0 – 15; Serve: 6

Ingredients:

- 12 prawns
- 2 eggs
- Flour to taste
- Breadcrumbs
- 1 tsp oil

Direction:

1. Remove the head of the prawns and shell carefully.
2. Pass the prawns first in the flour, then in the beaten egg and then in the breadcrumbs.
3. Preheat the air fryer for 1 minute at 150^0C.
4. Add the prawns and cook for 4 minutes. If the prawns are large, it will be necessary to cook 6 at a time.
5. Turn the prawns and cook for another 4 minutes.
6. They should be served with a yogurt or mayonnaise sauce.

Nutrition Value (Amount per Serving):

- Calories 2385.1
- Fat 23
- Carbohydrates 52.3g
- Sugar 0.1g
- Protein 21.4g

Mussels with Pepper

Preparation time: 10 - 20, Cooking time: 0 – 15; Serve: 6

Ingredients:

- 700g mussels
- 1 clove garlic
- 1 tsp oil
- Pepper to taste
- Parsley Taste

Direction:

1. Clean and scrape the mold cover and remove the byssus (the "beard" that comes out of the mold).

2. Pour the oil, clean the mussels and the crushed garlic in the basket. Set the temperature to 200^0C and simmer for 12 minutes. Towards the end of cooking, add black pepper and chopped parsley.

3. Finally, distribute the mussel juice well at the bottom of the basket, stirring the basket.

Nutrition Value (Amount per Serving):

- Calories 150
- Carbohydrates 2g
- Fat 8g
- Sugars 0g
- Protein 15g
- Cholesterol 0mg

Scallops in Butter with Leaves

Preparation time: 10 - 20, Cooking time: 15 - 30, 4 people, Calories: 127

Ingredients:

- 400g scallops
- 20g butter
- 1 clove garlic
- Leafs to taste
- Pepper to taste
- Parsley to taste
- ½ lemon juice

Direction:

1. Clean the scallops and dry them on a paper towel.
2. Place the butter and chopped garlic inside the basket. Set the temperature to 150^0C.
3. Melt the butter for 2 to 3 minutes.
4. Add the scallops, salt, pepper and cook for 8 minutes.
5. Then add the lemon juice, parsley, and finish cooking for another 3 to 4 minutes.
6. Very good as an appetizer to serve inside the shells.

Nutrition Value (Amount per Serving):

- Calories 315.6
- Fat 13.8 g
- Carbohydrate 11.0 g
- Sugars 0.1 g
- Protein 38.7 g
- Cholesterol 114.8 mg

Scallops in Butter

Preparation time: 10 - 20, Cooking time: 15 - 30, 4 people, Calories: 127

Ingredients:

- 400 g Scallops
- 20 g butter
- 1 clove garlic
- Salt to taste
- Pepper to taste
- Parsley to taste
- ½ lemon juice

Direction:

1. Remove the scallops by deciphering them, clean them and put them to dry on a paper towel.
2. Heat the air fryer at 150^0C for 5 minutes.
3. Melt the butter for 2 to 3 minutes.
4. Add the scallops, salt, pepper and cook for 8 minutes.
5. Then add the lemon juice, parsley, and finish cooking for another 3 to 4 minutes.
6. Very good as an appetizer to serve inside the shells.

Nutrition Value (Amount per Serving):

- Calories 315.6
- Fat 13.8 g
- Carbohydrate 11.0 g
- Sugars 0.1 g
- Protein 38.7 g
- Cholesterol 114.8 mg

Monkfish with Olives and Capers

Preparation time: 10 – 20; Cooking time: 30 – 45; Serve: 4

Ingredients:

- 1 monkfish
- 10 cherry tomatoes
- 50 g cailletier olives
- 5 capers

Direction:

1. Spread aluminum foil inside the basket and place the monkfish clean and skinless.
2. Add chopped tomatoes, olives, capers, oil, and salt.
3. Set the temperature to 160^0C.
4. Cook the monkfish for about 40 minutes (depending on the size of the fish).

Nutrition Value (Amount per Serving):

- Calories 404
- Fat 29g
- Carbohydrates 36g
- Sugars 7g
- Protein 24g
- Cholesterol 36mg

Shrimp, Zucchini and Cherry Tomato Sauce

Preparation time: 0-10, Cooking time: 15-30; Serve: 4

Ingredients:

- 2 zucchinis
- 300 shrimp
- 7 cherry tomatoes
- Pepper to taste
- Salt to taste
- 1 clove garlic

Direction:

1. Pour the oil, add the garlic clove and diced zucchini.
2. Cook for 15 minutes at 150^0C.
3. Add the shrimp and the pieces of tomato, salt, and spices.
4. Cook for another 5 to 10 minutes or until the shrimp water evaporates.

Nutrition Value (Amount per Serving):

- Calories 214.3
- Fat 8.6g
- Carbohydrate 7.8g
- Sugars 4.8g
- Protein 27.0g
- Cholesterol 232.7mg

Spinach Crusted Salmon

Preparation time: 10-20, Cooking time: 30-45; Serve; 6

Ingredients:

- 350 g salmon fillet
- 200 g bleached spinach
- 20g pine nuts
- 2 rolls of puff pastry
- 20 g butter
- 1 clove garlic
- Salt to taste
- Pepper to taste
- 1 egg

Direction:

1. Place the salmon, previously salted and spicy in the basket.
2. Cook for 15 minutes at 150^0C. Once cooked, remove the salmon from the basket and let it cool. Put the butter, garlic clove, spinach (previously bleached), pine nuts, sole and pepper, and cook for 5 minutes.
3. Unwind the puff pastry on a work surface. Place the fillet in the center of the puff pastry (the skin will have been removed before the fillet has cooled) and cover with the earlier preparation.
4. Brush the 4 sides with the beaten egg and then cover with the other puff pastry. Pinch the sides to adhere the two pastes. Cut the excess puff pastry. Make a chimney on top of the puff pastry to facilitate the release of steam during cooking, then brush it with the egg.
5. Place the liner at the bottom of the basket on the baking paper (without the mixing).
6. Cook for 20/25 minutes depending on the degree of browning desired. Let cool before slicing.

Nutrition Value (Amount per Serving):

- Calories 186
- Fat 8.24g
- Carbohydrates 4.87g
- Sugars 3.22g
- Protein 23.67g
- Cholesterol 80mg

Salmon with Pistachio Bark

Preparation time: 10 - 20, Cooking time: 15 – 30; Serve: 4

Ingredients:

- 600 g salmon fillet
- 50g pistachios
- Salt to taste

Direction:

1. Place the parchment paper on the bottom of the basket and place the salmon fillet in it (it can be cooked whole or already divided into four portions).
2. Cut the pistachios in thick pieces; grease the top of the fish, salt (little because the pistachios are already salted) and cover everything with the pistachios.
3. Set the air fryer to 180^0C and simmer for 25 minutes.

Nutrition Value (Amount per Serving):

- Calories 371.7
- Fat 21.8 g
- Carbohydrate 9.4 g
- Sugars 2.2g
- Protein 34.7 g
- Cholesterol 80.5 mg

Salmon in Papillote With Orange

Preparation time: 10 - 20, Cooking time: 15 – 30; Serve: 4

Ingredients:

- 600g salmon fillet
- 4 oranges
- Salt to taste
- 2 cloves of garlic
- Chives to taste
- 1 lemon

Direction:

1. Pour the freshly squeezed orange juice, the lemon juice, the zest of the two oranges into a bowl. Add two tablespoons of oil, salt, and garlic. Dip the previously washed salmon fillet and leave it in the marinade for one hour, preferably in the refrigerator
2. Place the steak and part of your marinade on a sheet of foil. Salt and sprinkle with chives and a few slices of orange.
3. Set to 160^0C. Simmer for 30 minutes. Open the sheet, let it evaporate and serve with a nice garnish of fresh orange.

Nutrition Value (Amount per Serving):

- Calories 229
- Fat 11g
- Carbohydrates 5g
- Sugar 3g
- Protein 25g
- Cholesterol 62mg

Salted Marinated Salmon

Preparation time: 0-10, Cooking time: 15-30; Serve: 2

Ingredients:

- 500g salmon fillet
- 1 kg coarse salt

Direction:

1. Place the baking paper on the basket and the salmon on top (skin side up) covered with coarse salt.
2. Set the air fryer to 150^0C.
3. Cook everything for 25 to 30 minutes. At the end of cooking, remove the salt from the fish and serve with a drizzle of oil.

Nutrition Value (Amount per Serving):

- Calories 290
- Fat 13g
- Carbohydrates 3g
- Fiber 0g
- Protein 40g
- Cholesterol 196mg

Sautéed Trout with Almonds

Preparation time: more than 30, Cooking time: 15 – 30; Serve:

Ingredients:

- 700 g salmon trout
- 15 black peppercorns
- Dill leaves to taste
- 30g almonds
- Salt to taste

Direction:

1. Cut the trout into cubes and marinate it for half an hour with the rest of the ingredients (except salt).
2. Cook for 17 minutes at 160^0C. Pour a drizzle of oil and serve.

Nutrition Value (Amount per Serving):

- Calories 238.5
- Fat 20.1 g
- Carbohydrate 11.5 g
- Sugars 1.0 g
- Protein 4.0 g
- Cholesterol 45.9 mg

Stuffed Cuttlefish

Preparation time: 10 - 20, Cooking time: 15 – 30; Serve: 4

Ingredients:

- 8 small cuttlefish
- 50 g of breadcrumbs
- Garlic to taste
- Parsley to taste
- 1 egg
- Salt to taste
- Pepper to taste

Direction:

1. Clean the cuttlefish, cut, and separate the tentacles. In a blender, pour the breadcrumbs, the parsley (without the branches), the egg, the salt, a drizzle of olive oil and the sepia tentacles.
2. Blend until you get a dense mixture. Fill the sepia with the mixture obtained.
3. Place the cuttlefish in the bowl.
4. Set the air fryer to 150^0C and cook for 20 minutes. At the end of cooking, add a drizzle of olive oil and serve.

Nutrition Value (Amount per Serving):

- Calories 67.1
- Fat 0.6g
- Carbohydrates 0.7g
- Protein 13.8g
- Cholesterol 95.2mg

Sicilian Tuna Slices

Preparation time: 10 - 20, Cooking time: 15 – 30; Serve: 4

Ingredients:

- 600 g of tuna slices
- 1 red onion stumbles
- 200 g chopped tomato
- 50 g boneless black olives
- 20 g desalted capers
- Salt to taste
- Pepper to taste
- Parsley to taste

Direction:

1. Pour sliced onion, tomato, olives, and capers in the basket.
2. Set the temperature to 150^0C and cook for 10 minutes.
3. Mix the sauce with a wooden spoon and add the slices of tuna, salt, and pepper.
4. Cook the fish for 10 minutes, turning it halfway through cooking.
5. Dress with chopped parsley.

Nutrition Value (Amount per Serving):

- Calories 233
- Carbohydrates 12g
- Fat 6g
- Sugars 0g
- Protein 29g
- Cholesterol 51 mg

Fish in Air Fryer

Preparation time: 5 minutes; Cooking time: 10 minutes; Serve: 1

Ingredients:

- 1 lemon juice
- 3 fish fillets
- 1 tbsp full seasoning with achiote
- 1 tbsp ground garlic
- 1 tbsp ground onion
- Chickpea flour needed
- Water

Direction:

1. Rinse the fish. And cut them into pieces. Dry with paper towels. Spread with lemon and season.
2. In a bowl add the chickpea flour and little water to form a thick cream.
3. Batter the fish pieces. Spread the pan of the fryer with oil and place the fish. Cook for 10 minutes at 160^0C.
4. Also, the cooking time will depend on the equipment you use.

Nutrition Value (Amount per Serving):

- Calories 280
- Fat 12.5g
- Carbohydrates 0g
- Fiber 0g
- Sugars 0g
- Protein 39.2g

Rabas

Preparation time: 5 minutes; Cooking time: 12 minutes; Serve: 4

Ingredients:

- 16 rabas
- 1 egg
- Breadcrumbs
- Salt, pepper, sweet paprika

Direction:

1. Put the rabas boil for 2 minutes.
2. Remove and dry well.
3. Beat the egg and season to taste. You can put salt, pepper and sweet paprika. Place in the egg.
4. Bread with breadcrumbs. Place in sticks.
5. Place in the fryer 5 minutes at 160^0C. Remove
6. Spray with a cooking spray and place 5 more minutes at 200^0C.

Nutrition Value (Amount per Serving):

- Calories 200
- Fat 1g
- Carbohydrates 1g
- Sugars 0g
- Protein 1g
- Cholesterol 0mg

Prawns in Ham with Red Pepper Sauce

Preparation time: 15 minutes; Cooking time: 13 minutes; Serve: 5

Ingredients:

- 1 red bell pepper cut in half
- 10 prawns (frozen), already thawed
- 5 slices of ham
- 1 tbsp olive oil
- 1 clove garlic, minced
- ½ tbsp paprika
- Freshly ground black pepper

Direction:

1. Preheat the air fryer to 200°C. Place the pepper in the basket and place it in the air fryer. Set the timer to 10 minutes. Roast the pepper until the skin is slightly burned. Place the pepper in a bowl and cover it with a lid or with transparent film. Let stand about 15 minutes.

2. Peel the prawns, make an incision in the back, and remove the black vein. Divide the slices of ham into two halves lengthwise and roll each shrimp into a slice of ham.

3. Apply a thin layer of olive oil to the packets and place them in the basket. Insert it into the air fryer and set the timer to 3 minutes. Fry the prawns until they are crispy and ready.

4. Meanwhile, peel the halves of peppers, remove the seeds, and chop them. Beat them in the blender together with the garlic, paprika and olive oil. Pour the sauce on a plate and season with salt and pepper to taste.

5. Serve the prawns with ham on skewers and add a small plate with the red pepper sauce.

Nutrition Value (Amount per Serving):

- Calories 187
- Fat 17g
- Carbohydrates 9g
- Fiber 2g
- Sugar 2g
- Protein 2g

Chapter 4

Poultry

Chopped Chicken Olive Tomato Sauce

Preparation time: 10 minutes; Cooking time: 30 minutes; Serve: 4

Ingredients:

- 500 g chicken cutlet
- 2 minced shallots+1 degermed garlic clove
- 75 g of tomato sauce + 15 g of 30% liquid cream
- 1 bay leaf+salt+pepper+1 tsp Provence herbs
- 20 pitted green and black olives

Direction:

1. Cut the chicken cutlets into strips and put them in the fryer basket with the garlic and the shallots. Do not put oil. Salt/pepper.
2. Set the timer and the temperature to 10-12 minutes at 200°C
3. Add the tomato sauce, the cream, the olives, the bay leaf, and the Provence herbs. Salt if necessary. Mix with a wooden spoon.
4. Close the air fryer and program 20 minutes at 180°C.
5. Eat hot with rice or pasta.

Nutrition Value (Amount per Serving):

- Calories 220.2
- Fat 7.0 g
- Carbohydrate 8.5 g
- Sugars 4.5 g
- Protein 28.9 g
- Cholesterol 114.8 mg

Chicken Thighs in Coconut Sauce, Nuts

Preparation time: 10 minutes; Cooking time: 30 minutes; Serve: 4

Ingredients:

- 8 skinless chicken thighs
- 2 chopped onions
- 25 ml of coconut cream + 100 ml of coconut milk
- 4 tbsp coconut powder + 1 handful of dried fruit mix+ 5 dried apricots, diced + a few cashew nuts and almonds
- Fine salt + pepper

Direction:

1. Put the onions, chopped with the chicken thighs, in the air fryer (without oil). Add salt and pepper. Program 10 minutes at 200°C.
2. Stir alone with a wooden spoon.
3. Add coconut cream and milk, coconut powder, dried fruits, and apricots. Get out if necessary. Continue cooking by programming 20 minutes at 200°C. You don't have anything to do; it cooks alone, without any problem.
4. With the tongs, remove the bowl and serve hot with rice, vegetables, Chinese noodles............... A delight. Perfect kitchen

Nutrition Value (Amount per Serving):

- Calories 320.4
- Fat 11.6 g
- Carbohydrate 9.0 g
- Sugars 2.1 g
- Protein 44.0 g
- Cholesterol 102.7 mg

Forest Guinea Hen

Preparation time: about 15 minutes; Cooking time: 1 h 15 - 1 h 30; Serve: 4

Ingredients:

- A beautiful guinea fowl farm weighing 1 to 1.5 kilos
- 100g of dried or fresh porcini mushrooms according to the season
- 8 large potatoes Béa
- 1 plate
- 2 cloves of garlic
- 1 shallot
- Chopped parsley
- A pinch of butter
- Vegetable oil
- Salt and pepper

Direction:

1. Put the dried mushrooms in water to rehydrate them or simply clean them if they are fresh porcini mushrooms. Peel the potatoes and cut them finely. Chop the garlic and parsley and set aside.
2. Prepare the guinea fowl by cutting the neck and removing all the giblets inside. Garnish with stuffed dough, garlic cloves and parsley.
3. Place guinea fowls in the air fryer at 200^{0}C without oil of sufficient capacity. Simply add the butter knob and a tablespoon of cooking oil. Allow approximately one hour of cooking per kilo, so you will have to check after a certain period.
4. When the guinea fowl is ready, prepare the porcini mushrooms in the oil-free fryer by adding the shallot. This preparation is very fast, and you should not forget salt and pepper.
5. When everything is ready, place each of the preparations in the air fryer, sprinkle with the cooking juices and cook for another 15 minutes.
6. Serve hot to enjoy all the flavors of the dish.

Nutrition Value (Amount per Serving):

- Calories 110
- Fat 2.5g
- Carbohydrate 0g
- Sugars 0g
- Protein 21g
- Cholesterol 63mg

Fried and Crispy Chicken

Preparation time: 15 minutes; Cooking time: 35-40 minutes; Serve: 4

Ingredients:

- 4 chicken breasts
- 1 tbsp olive oil
- 1 tbsp breadcrumbs
- 1 tbsp of a spice mixture
- Salt
- 250g of potatoes per person

Direction:

1. Cut chicken breasts into 4 slices
2. Mix them with the other ingredients so that the chicken is perfectly covered with the preparation.
3. Peel and cut the potatoes in the same way as the fries, trying to make a regular cut to cook better.
4. Place the strips in the air fryer without oil and cook at 200^0C for 15 to 20 minutes to get a crispy chicken.
5. For French fries, wait 30 minutes to cook.

Nutrition Value (Amount per Serving):

- Calories 227
- Carbohydrates 23g
- Fat 18g
- Sugars 0g
- Protein 12g
- Cholesterol 63mg

Orange Turkey Bites

Preparation time: 10-20; Cooking time: 15-30; Serve: 8

Ingredients:

- 750 g turkey
- 1 shallot
- 2 oranges
- Thyme to taste
- 1 tsp oil
- Salt and pepper to taste

Direction:

1. Cut the turkey into pieces and peel the oranges, cutting the skin into strips.
2. Put the chopped shallot, the orange peel, the thyme, and the oil in the basket of the preheated air fryer at 150 for 5 minutes. Brown all for 4 min.
3. Add ½ glass of water, lightly floured turkey, salt, and pepper; simmer for 6 more minutes.
4. Then add the orange juice and cook at 200^0C for 15 minutes until a thick juice is obtained.
5. Serve garnished with some thyme leaves and slices of orange.

Nutrition Value (Amount per Serving):

- Calories 80
- Fat 5g
- Carbohydrates 1g
- Sugar 0g
- Protein 7g
- Cholesterol 25mg

Chicken Thighs with Potatoes

Preparation time: 0-10; Cooking time: 45-60; Serve: 6

Ingredients:

- 1kg chicken thighs
- 800g of potatoes in pieces
- Salt to taste
- Pepper to taste
- Rosemary at ease
- 1 clove garlic

Direction:

1. Preheat the air fryer at 180^0C for 15 minutes.
2. Place the chicken thighs in the basket and add the previously peeled and washed potatoes, add a clove of garlic, rosemary sprigs, salt, and pepper.
3. Set the temperature 200^0C and cook everything for 50 min. Mix 3-4 times during cooking (when they are well browned on the surface) and chicken 1-2 times.

Nutrition Value (Amount per Serving):

- Calories 419.4
- Fat 9.5 g
- Carbohydrate 44.8 g
- Sugars 2.0 g
- Protein 39.1 g
- Cholesterol 115.8 mg

Chicken Blanquette With Soy

Preparation time: 10-20; Cooking time: 15-30; Serve:

Ingredients:

- 600g Chicken breast
- 300g Potatoes
- 100g Bean sprouts
- 150g Broth
- 50g Onion
- 1tsp Olive oil
- 25g Soy sauce

Direction:

1. Cut the meat and potatoes into pieces.
2. Pour the sliced oil and onion into the bottom of the tank, close the lid.
3. Set the air fryer at 150^0C to brown for 5 minutes.
4. Add the floured chicken, potatoes, broth, salt, and pepper and cook for another 13 minutes.
5. Then pour the sprouts and the soy sauce and cook for another 10 minutes.

Nutrition Value (Amount per Serving):

- Calories 250
- Carbohydrates 19g
- Fat 11g
- Sugars 7g
- Protein 16g
- Cholesterol 0mg

Fish Sticks

Cooking time: 15-30; Serve: 6

Ingredients:

- 18 pieces Fish patties

Direction:

1. Remove the mixing paddle from the tank.
2. Heat the air fryer at 150^0C for 5 minutes
3. Cook everything for 20 min.

Nutrition Value (Amount per Serving):

- Calories 281
- Total Fat 15 g
- Carbohydrates 23.9 g
- Sugars 2.8 g
- Protein 12.5 g
- Cholesterol 36 mg

Vegetarian Curry with Pumpkin and Chickpeas

Preparation time: 20-30; Cooking time: 15-30; Serve: 6

Ingredients:

- 600g pumpkin, cleaned
- 300g chicken weights already cooked
- 1 tsp oil
- 1 tsp paprika
- 1 tsp curry
- ½ onion
- 1 clove garlic
- 1 tsp tomato puree
- 200 ml of broth
- 1 tsp turmeric
- 480g basmati rice

Direction:

1. Remove the skin of the pumpkin and the seeds inside. Cut it into small pieces, the same size as the chickpeas to have the same cooking time.
2. Pour the chopped onion and garlic, oil, and spices (paprika - curry - turmeric - saffron) in the basket.
3. Set the temperature to 150^0C and brown all for 4 min.
4. Add the pumpkin and brown for 6 min. additional.
5. Then pour the chickpeas, tomato puree, broth and cook for 10 min. additional.
6. Meanwhile, boil basmati rice in saltwater, drain and serve with vegetarian curry.

Nutrition Value (Amount per Serving):

- Calories 249.6
- Fat 11.7 g
- Carbohydrate 27.8 g
- Sugars 9.6 g
- Protein 8.1 g
- Cholesterol 0.0 mg

Turkey Diced with Ginger, Apples and Vegetables

Preparation time: 10-20; Cooking time: 30-45; Serve: 4

Ingredients:

- 600g turkey breast
- 150g carrots
- 100g of celery
- 50g onion
- 200g of potatoes
- Ginger to taste
- Flour at discretion
- 200ml broth
- 1 tsp olive oil
- Leave at discretion
- Black pepper to taste
- 1 apple

Direction:

1. Preheat the air fryer at 150°C for 5 minutes.
2. Cut the meat and vegetables into small pieces.
3. Pour the sliced oil and onion into the bottom of the basket and cook for 5 minutes.
4. Add carrots, celery, potatoes, and broth, then cook for another 15 minutes.
5. Add the floured turkey, salt, and pepper, then cook for another 15 minutes (if necessary, add some water).
6. Add the apple pieces and ginger at the end and continue cooking for another 5 minutes.

Nutrition Value (Amount per Serving):

- Fat 13.6g
- Carbohydrates 2.3g
- Sugars 0g
- Protein 42.4g
- Cholesterol 124.9mg Value (Amount per Serving):

Ligurian Rabbit

Preparation time: 10-20, Cooking time: 45-60, 6 people, Calories: 440

Ingredients:

- 1 kg of rabbit pieces
- 150g green olives
- 2 tbsp pine nuts
- 100ml broth
- 1 shallot
- 1 clove garlic
- 1 rosemary branch
- 1 glass of red wine
- 1 tsp olive oil
- 2-3 bay leaves
- Salt to taste

Direction:

1. Put the chopped onion, oil, and garlic in the basket. Set the temperature to 200^0C and brown for 2 min.
2. Add meat, red wine and cook for another 8 min.
3. Finally add the green olives, pine nuts, broth, herbs, salt and pepper and simmer for another 50 min. (until the rabbit becomes tender, the meat should easily detach from the bone) turning 2-3 times (if the bottom is too dry, add the broth).

Nutrition Value (Amount per Serving):

- Calories 795
- Fat 8g
- Carbohydrates 0g
- Sugars 0g
- Protein 20.8g
- Cholesterol 82mg

Frozen Chicken Nuggets

Cooking time: 15-30; Serve: 8

Ingredients:

- 750 g of frozen chicken nuggets
- Fine salt to taste

Direction:

1. Pour the chicken nuggets in the basket
2. Cook for 18 min at 200^0C.
3. Salt and serve.

Nutrition Value (Amount per Serving):

- Calories 33
- Fat 1g
- Carbohydrates 2.8g
- Sugar 0g
- Protein 3.3g
- Cholesterol 9mg

Chicken with Cacciatore (Chicken Hunter)

Preparation time: 10-20, Cooking time: 30-45; Serve: 6

Ingredients:

- 1 kg of chicken pieces
- 1 onion:
- 2 carrots
- 3 celery stalks
- 1 clove garlic
- 1 glass of red wine
- 400 g peeled tomatoes
- 50 g of olives
- Salt, pepper, parsley to taste

Direction:

1. Clean the chicken and place it inside the basket previously greased with the cooking spray.
2. Set the temperature to 180^0C and cook the chicken pieces for 15 minutes.
3. Add the celery mince, carrots, onions, garlic, red wine, salt, pepper, and simmer for an additional 5 minutes.
4. Then pour the tomato and olives and finish simmering for additional 20 minutes stirring chicken and sauce.
5. Once cooked, add a handful of chopped parsley, and serve hot with mash or polenta.

Nutrition Value (Amount per Serving):

- Calories 233
- Fat 7g
- 10g carbohydrates
- Sugars 2.2g
- Protein 34.7g
- Cholesterol 98.5mg

Devil Chicken

Preparation time: 10-20, Cooking time: 45-60; Serve: 4

Ingredients:

- 1 kg of whole chicken
- Salt to taste
- Black pepper to taste
- Chili pepper

Direction:

1. Thoroughly clean the chicken and cut it along the white. Flatten it well on the work surface and then massage with oil and spices.
2. Cook the chicken for 35 minutes at 200^0C.
3. Turn the chicken and cook another 25 minutes.

Nutrition Value (Amount per Serving):

- Calories 429.7
- Fat 17.3 g
- Carbohydrate 19.5 g
- Sugars 5.1 g
- Protein 51.1 g
- Cholesterol 155.0 mg

Chicken with Pineapple

Preparation time: 10 - 20, Cooking time: 15 – 30; Serve: 6

Ingredients:

- 600g chicken breast
- 350 g canned pineapple
- 50 ml pineapple juice
- 1 tbsp of starch
- ½ tbsp ginger
- ½ tbsp curry
- 15 ml soy sauce
- Salt to taste
- Pepper to taste
- Flour (sufficient quantity)

Direction:

1. The floured chicken cut into small pieces, salt, and pepper in the basket previously greased.
2. Simmer for 8 minutes at 180^0C (If, at the end of cooking, the chicken pieces stick together, separate them with a wooden spoon).
3. Add the pineapple into small pieces, ginger and curry and simmer for added 3 minutes.
4. Finally, add water, soy sauce and diluted starch to pineapple juice. Simmer for another 6 minutes until the sauce has thickened.
5. Ideal accompanied with basmati rice.

Nutrition Value (Amount per Serving):

- Calories 222
- Fat 7.1g
- Carbohydrates 11g
- Sugars 9.7g
- Protein 27g
- Cholesterol 85mg

Chicken Curry

Preparation time: 10-20, Cooking time: 15-30; Serve: 6

Ingredients:

- 600g chicken breast
- 1 onion
- 2 carrots
- 150 ml
- 200 ml of fresh cream
- 100 ml of milk
- Salt to taste
- 2 spoons of curry
- Flour 00 (sufficient quantity)

Direction:

1. Chop the onion in a food processor and cut the carrots into cubes or slices.
2. Spray the basket and distribute the onion and carrots evenly in the basket.
3. Brown for 5 minutes at 150^0C.
4. Add the floured chicken, cut into small pieces, the broth, salt, and simmer for another 5 min.
5. Finally pour the fresh cream, the milk and finish cooking for another 15 min. Ideal accompanied with basmati rice.

Nutrition Value (Amount per Serving):

- Calories 243
- Fat 11g
- Carbohydrates 7.5g
- Sugars 2g
- Protein 28g
- Cholesterol 74mg

Chicken with Yogurt and Mustard

Preparation time: 10 - 20, Cooking time: 15 – 30; 6

Ingredients:

- 500 g chicken breast
- 100 g of white yogurt
- 40 g mustard
- 1 shallot
- Salt to taste
- Pepper to taste

Direction:

1. Place the chopped shallot inside the basket previously greased.
2. Brown for 3 minutes at 150^0C
3. Add the chicken pieces, salt, pepper and cook for another 15 minutes at 180^0C.
4. Then pour the mustard and yogurt and cook for another 5 minutes.

Nutrition Value (Amount per Serving):

- Calories 287.1
- Fat 8.9g
- Carbohydrate 4.3 g
- Sugars 1.7 g
- Protein 43.6 g
- Cholesterol 99.9 mg

Almond Chicken

Preparation time: 10 - 20, Cooking time: 15 – 30; 6

Ingredients:

- 500 g chicken breast
- 130g crushed almonds
- ½ onion
- 1 tbsp grated fresh ginger
- 60 g of soy sauce
- Water (sufficient quantity)

Direction:

1. Pour the almonds into the basket.
2. Roast the almonds for 5 minutes at 150^0C.
3. Remove the almonds and pour the chopped onion and ginger, the oil into the tank and brown for about 2 minutes.
4. Add lightly floured chicken, salt, pepper and cook for additional 13 minutes.
5. Pour the soy sauce, a ladle of hot water, the roasted almonds and simmer for additional 5 minutes.

Nutrition Value (Amount per Serving):

- Calories 458
- Fat 34g
- Carbohydrates 22g
- Sugars 7.3g
- Protein 20g
- Cholesterol 24mg

Mushroom Chicken

Preparation time: 10-20, Cooking time: 15-30; Serve: 6

Ingredients:

- 500 g chicken breast
- Mushroom 300g
- 100 g of fresh cream
- 1 shallot

Direction:

1. Cut the chicken into pieces and sliced mushrooms. Spray the basket and chopped shallot into the basket. Set the temperature to 150^0C and lightly brown for 5 minutes.
2. Add the mushrooms and cook for additional 6 minutes.
3. Finally pour the chicken, salt, pepper, and simmer for another 10 minutes.
4. Then add the fresh cream and cook for 5 min. until the sauce has thickened.

Nutrition Value (Amount per Serving):

- Calories 220
- Fat 14g
- Carbohydrates 11g
- Sugar 4g
- Protein 12g
- Cholesterol 50mg

Pepper Chicken

Preparation time: 10-20; Cooking time: 45-60; Serve: 6

Ingredients:

- 1 kg of chicken pieces
- 500 g of red and yellow peppers
- Salt to taste
- 50g onion

Direction:

1. Pour the chopped onion into the bowl with the chopped peppers and chicken. Add salt and pepper.
2. Set the temperature to 150^0C.
3. Cook everything for about 50 minutes, mixing 3 to 4 times during cooking, both meat and peppers.

Nutrition Value (Amount per Serving):

- Calories 281
- Fat 12g
- Carbohydrates 21g
- Sugars 3.4g
- Protein 23g
- Cholesterol 102mg

Stuffed Chicken and Baked Potatoes

Preparation time: 10-20, Cooking time: 45-60; Serve: 4

Ingredients:

- 800 g boneless chicken
- 300 g minced meat
- 150 g sausage
- 80 g French toast
- 1 tbsp chopped parsley

Direction:

1. Bone the chicken (or bone directly by the butcher).

Prepare the filling:

2. Put in a food processor the meat, the sausage, the French toast bathed in milk to soften it, the parsley, the eggs, the grated cheese, the salt, the pepper and mix until obtaining a homogeneous and compact mixture.
3. Fill the boneless chicken and tie it well with a kitchen rope so that the filling does not come out.
4. Place the chicken inside the bowl, add the chopped potatoes, oil, salt, and pepper.
5. Set the air fryer to 160^0C. Cook everything for 60 minutes over mix the potatoes 2-3 times to cook evenly and turn the chicken about once in the middle of cooking.

Nutrition Value (Amount per Serving):

- Calories 223.8
- Fat 6.5 g
- Carbohydrate 19.8 g
- Sugars 1.9 g
- Protein 21.2 g
- Cholesterol 48.8 mg

Tandoori Chicken

Preparation time: more than 30, Cooking time: 15 – 30; Serve: 4

Ingredients:

- 600 g chicken pieces
- 125 g whole yogurt
- 1 tbsp curry
- 3 tsp of spices for roasted meats

Direction:

1. Place all ingredients in a bowl, flame well and let stand for 1 hour in the refrigerator.
2. Place the pieces of meat in the basket and set the temperature to 160^0C
3. Cook the meat for 30 minutes, turning it 1-2 times to brown the chicken on both sides.

Nutrition Value (Amount per Serving):

- Calories 263
- Fat 12g
- Carbohydrates 6.1g
- Sugars 3.7g
- Protein 31g
- Cholesterol 135mg

Crispy Chicken Fillets in Brine in Pickle Juice

Preparation time: 10 minutes; Cooking time: 12 minutes; Serve: 4

Ingredients:

- 12 chicken offers (1 ¼ pounds in total)
- 1 ¼ cups pickled dill juice
- 1 large egg
- 1 large egg white
- ½ tsp kosher salt
- Freshly ground black pepper
- ½ cup seasoned breadcrumbs, regular or gluten free
- ½ cup seasoned breadcrumbs, regular or gluten free
- Olive oil spray

Direction:

1. Place the chicken in a shallow bowl and cover with the pickle juice (enough to cover completely). Cover and marine for 8 hours in the refrigerator.
2. Drain the chicken and dry it completely with a paper towel (discard the marinade). In a medium bowl, beat the whole egg, egg white, salt, and pepper. In a shallow arch, combine the breadcrumbs.
3. Dip the chicken in the egg mixture, piece by piece, then in the breadcrumbs, pressing lightly. Remove excess breadcrumbs and place it on a work surface. Spray generously both sides of the chicken with oil.
4. Preheat the fryer to 400°F.
5. Working in batches, place a single layer of chicken in the fryer basket. Cook 10 to 12 minutes, turning halfway through cooking, until cooked, crispy and golden brown. (For a toaster-style air fryer, the temperature stays the same; cook for about 10 minutes.)

Nutrition Value (Amount per Serving):

- Calories: 244kcal
- Carbohydrates 10g
- Protein: 37g
- Fat: 6g
- Cholesterol 150mg
- Sugar 1g

Chapter 5

Beef, Pork, Lamb Recipes

Perfect Garlic Butter Steak

Preparation: 20 min. – Cooking time: 12 min.

Ingredients:

- 2 Ribeye steaks
- Salt
- Pepper
- Olive oil
- Garlic butter:
- ½ cup softened butter
- 2 tbsp chopped fresh parsley
- 2 garlic cloves, minced
- 1 tsp Worcestershire sauce
- ½ tsp salt (optional)

Direction:

1. Prepare the garlic butter by mixing all the ingredients together.
2. Place in parchment paper. Roll up and put in the fridge.
3. Let the steaks sit for 20 minutes at room temperature.
4. Brush with a little oil, salt, and pepper.
5. Preheat your hot air fryer to 400°F (200°C).
6. Cook for 12 minutes, turning halfway through cooking. Serve.
7. Place the garlic butter on the steaks and let sit for 5 minutes.
8. Enjoy!

Nutrition Value (Amount per Serving):

- Calories 250
- Fat 10g
- Carbohydrates 2g
- Sugars 1g
- Protein 36g
- Cholesterol 100mg

Crispy Pork Medallions

Preparation time: 20 minutes; Cooking time: 5 minutes; Serve: 2

Ingredients:

- 1 pork loin, 330 g, cut into 6 or 7 slices of 4 cm
- 1 tsp Dijon mustard
- 1 tsp oil
- Salt, pepper and paprika
- Asian marinade
- 1 tsp salt reduced tamari sauce
- 1 tsp olive oil
- 1 clementine juice
- 1 pinch cayenne pepper
- 2 cloves garlic, pressed
- Crunchy coating
- 1/3 cup breadcrumbs
- ½ orange zest
- 2g freshly grated Parmesan cheese

Direction:

1. Prepare the marinade first. In a bowl, combine all the ingredients. Lightly salt the medallions, pepper, and sprinkle with paprika. Place these in the marinade and turn them several times to impregnate them completely. Cover with plastic wrap and marinate for 1 hour at room temperature.

2. Prepare the coating by combining the breadcrumbs, the orange zest, and the Parmesan cheese in a deep dish.

3. When the maceration time has elapsed, remove the marinade medallions, and dry them on absorbent paper. Spread with mustard, then move on to the crunchy layer. Brush lightly with oil.

4. Heat the air fryer to 350°F. Place the medallions in the fryer basket. Cook 5 minutes, stir, and then return to the fryer for another minute. Serve immediately.

Nutrition Value (Amount per Serving):

- Calories 222
- Carbohydrates 13g
- Fat 6g
- Protein 24g
- Sugars 0h
- Cholesterol 74mg

Nemos Beef with Dry Pepper Lactose Free

Preparation time: 30 minutes; Cooking time: 20-25 minutes; Serve: 5

Ingredients:

- 250g of minced meat
- 1 handful of rice noodles
- 25 rice leaves
- 1 small onion
- 1 clove garlic
- 1 cube of chicken broth
- Roasted Sesame Oil
- 2 tsp dried pepper
- 1 tbsp soy sauce
- 1 tsp ground ginger

Direction:

1. Finely chop the onion and garlic and mix with the minced meat. Add half of the dried pepper, being careful to crush it beforehand. Add the ginger powder and soy sauce. Brown the preparation in roasted sesame oil, making sure you only have small pieces of minced meat.
2. Bring a pan of boiling water to which you will add chicken broth. Dip the rice noodles in it for only 3 minutes.
3. Add them to the ground beef preparation and then add the rest of the dried pepper.
4. Lightly moisten the rice leaves, place the filling in the middle and close them to create a perfect nem.
5. Place the spring rolls in the air fryer without oil previously heated at 150^0C and cook for 10 to 15 minutes, according to taste.

Nutrition Value (Amount per Serving):

- Calories 203
- Carbohydrates 7g
- Fat 15g
- Protein 12g
- Sugars 5g
- Cholesterol 0mg

Pork and Parsni With Thai, Marinated with Honey and Soy

Preparation time: 20 minutes; Cooking time: 30 minutes; Serve: 2

Ingredients:

- 2 pork ribs to choose from the tenderloin
- 1 large parsnip
- 1 coriander leaf
- 1 sprig fresh chopped parsley
- Salt
- For the marinade:
- 2 tbsp olive oil
- 2 tbsp soy sauce
- The juice of half a lemon
- 1 tbsp of honey, preferably flavored with orange blossom
- 1 tsp of specific spices for wok preparation
- 1 tsp of Asian spice mix
- Coriander powder

Direction:

1. Prepare the marinade by mixing all the ingredients in a large bowl. Mix to obtain a very homogeneous mixture.
2. Dip the pork chunks in the marinade, turning them over to make sure it covers the meat ribs perfectly. Prepare the parsnip by peeling and washing it, and then cut it into small dice.
3. Use a large plate to place the pieces of pork and parsnips covered with marinade. Pour the parsnips into the bowl and mix. Let stand for at least 1 hour before cooking.
4. Set the air fryer at 160^0C without oil for 30 minutes and cook the parsnips.
5. At the end of the 10 minutes of cooking, add the pieces of pork or proceed to a traditional baking in the oven with 10 minutes on each side being careful to keep the cooking juices.

Nutrition Value (Amount per Serving):

- Calories 179
- Carbohydrates 11g
- Fat 13g
- Sugars 6g
- Protein 1g
- Cholesterol 0mg

Pork Fillet Mignon

Preparation time: 5 minutes; Cooking time: 12 minutes; Serve: 3

Ingredients:

- 6 medallions of 100g to 150g cut in a pork loin
- Olive oil
- Salt and pepper

Direction:

1. Cut six pork medallions the same size as the pork loin you own.
2. Salt and pepper to your liking.
3. Use a cooking tool to spray a very small amount of olive oil.
4. Place your pork medallions on the air fryer previously preheated at 150^{0}C and cook for 12 minutes.

Nutrition Value (Amount per Serving):

- Calories 125
- Fat 3.4g
- Carbohydrates 0g
- Sugars 0g
- Protein 22g
- Cholesterol 62mg

Lamb with Potatoes

Preparation time: 10-20 minutes; Cooking time: 30 - 45 minutes; Serve: 2

Ingredients:

- 1 kg Lamb milk in pieces
- 600g Fresh potatoes
- 5 spoons Sunflower oil
- Salt and pepper
- 2 spoons Sage, rosemary, thyme
- ½ glass White wine

Direction:

1. Remove the mixing paddle from the tank.
2. Put the pieces of lamb, oil, sage, rosemary, and thyme in the cooking pot. Close the cover, set the thermostat to position 4, press the lower resistance power key and press the on / off key; brown for 4 min.
3. Add the wine and simmer for another 6 min.
4. Preheat the air fryer at 150^0C for 5 minutes.
5. Finally pour the potatoes cut into pieces, salt, pepper and cook for 35 min. Extra by mixing the potatoes manually 2-3 times during cooking.

Nutrition Value (Amount per Serving):

- Calories 372.0
- Fat 12.3 g
- Carbohydrate 34.1 g
- Sugars 1.9
- Protein 31.5 g
- Cholesterol 86.7 mg

Veal Blanquette With Peas

Preparation time: 10-20; Cooking time: 45-60; Serve: 2

Ingredients:

- 600g Veal meat
- 250g Frozen peas
- ½ Onions
- ½ glass White wine
- 1 tsp Oil
- 250 ml Broth

Direction:

1. Chop the onion and put it inside the tank with the oil. Close the lid
2. Brown for 5 min setting the air fryer at 150^0C.
3. Add lightly floured meat, white wine, and simmer for 10 minutes.
4. Then add frozen peas, broth, salt, pepper, and simmer for 35 minutes. additional depending on the desired degree of cooking.

Nutrition Value (Amount per Serving):

- Calories 418
- Carbohydrates 24g
- Fat 14g
- Sugars 0g
- Protein 49g
- Cholesterol 357mg

Beef Stroganoff

Preparation time: 10-20; Cooking time: 15 – 30; Serve: 6

Ingredients:

- 1000 g beef
- 500g onion
- Mushrooms 500g
- 150g sour cream
- 50 g butter
- 100 g of broth
- Salt, pepper to taste
- 2 tbsp paprika
- Flour

Direction:

1. Cut the onion into very thin slices, then clean the mushrooms well and cut them into slices, finally cut the meat into strips about 5 cm long.
2. Place the butter, onion, and mushrooms on the baking sheet.
3. Preheat the air fryer at 200C for 5 minutes. Simmer for 10 min.
4. Add the floured meat, paprika, broth, salt, pepper, and simmer for another 10 minutes.
5. Finally pour the cream and finish cooking for another 5 minutes or until ready.

Nutrition Value (Amount per Serving):

- Calories 391
- Fat 23g
- Carbohydrates 21g
- Sugars 3.2g
- Protein 25g
- Cholesterol 115mg

Meatballs with Tomatoes and Peas

Preparation time: 10 – 20; Cooking time: 15 - 30, 6 people.

Ingredients:

- 425 g minced meat
- 1 egg
- 25 g grated cheese
- Salt to taste
- To taste breadcrumbs
- Parsley chopped to taste
- 150 g of frozen peas
- 400 g of tomatoes cut into large pieces
- 1 tsp oil
- 2 shallots

Direction:

1. Put the minced meat, the egg, the grated cheese, the salt, the parsley, the breadcrumbs in a bowl and mix until you get a consistent mixture. Form the meatballs (with these doses you will get 15-18 meatballs).
2. Chop the shallots and pour them into the basket greased with the oil. Close. Set the air fryer at 150^0C and brown for 3 min.
3. Add the meatballs and simmer for an additional 7 minutes.
4. Then add the frozen peas, tomato, salt and pepper and simmer for another 18 minutes.

Nutrition Value (Amount per Serving):

- Calories 40
- Fat 2.9 g
- Carbohydrates 0.9 g
- Sugars 0.5 g
- Protein 2.7 g
- Cholesterol 15 mg

Cevapi

Preparation time: more than 30; Cooking time: 15 – 30; Serve: 4

Ingredients:

- 150g of onion
- 350g ground beef
- 150g minced pork
- Leave at discretion
- Pepper at discretion
- Red paprika at discretion

Direction:

1. Mix all the ingredients in a bowl (the onion must be finely chopped) and knead well; form rolls 4 to 5 cm long and let stand in the refrigerator for at least 1 hour.
2. Place the cevapi in the basket of the air fryer. Set the temperature to 150^0C.
3. Cook the cevapis (8 at a time) for about 13 to 15 minutes, turning them in the middle of cooking.

Nutrition Value (Amount per Serving):

- Calories 63
- Fat 4.84g
- Carbohydrates 0.25g
- Sugars 0.02g
- Protein 4.19g
- Cholesterol 17mg

Milanese Chop

Preparation time: 10 – 20; Cooking time: 15 – 30; Serve: 2

Ingredients:

- 2 veal chops
- 1 egg
- 70 g of breadcrumbs
- Salt to taste
- 1 tsp oil

Direction:

1. Beat the egg in a bowl and prepare the breadcrumbs on a flat plate.
2. Pass each chop in the egg and then in breadcrumbs. Press the meat firmly into the pie. Put in the refrigerator for at least half an hour.
3. Pour the oil into the basket. Place the two chops.
4. Set the air fryer to 150^0 and cook the meat for 10 minutes and then turn the chop.
5. Cook for 5 minutes additional.
6. Serve the chops still hot, covering the bone with aluminum foil to facilitate tasting.

Nutrition Value (Amount per Serving):

- Calories 231
- Carbohydrates 8g
- Fat 9g
- Sugars 0g
- Protein 27g
- Cholesterol 97mg

Lemon Chops

Preparation time: 0-10; Cooking time: 0-15; Serve: 2

Ingredients:

- 4 slices of pork
- 40g butter
- Flour to taste
- 1 lemon juice
- Salt to taste

Direction:

1. Preheat the air fryer at 180°C for 5 minutes.
2. Flour the pork slices. Place the butter in the basket and brown for 2 minutes.
3. Add the previously floured and salted pork slices, simmer for 3 another minutes. Turn them on themselves.
4. Add the lemon juice and simmer for 3 another minutes.
5. Remove the slices and add a pinch of butter to the tank to thicken the juice. Mix the juice with a wooden spoon and pour the scallops over it.
6. Serve decorating the dish with lemon julienne.

Nutrition Value (Amount per Serving):

- Calories 242.4
- Fat 15.7 g
- Carbohydrate 0.7 g
- Sugars 0.0 g
- Protein 23.2 g
- Cholesterol 65.9 mg

Amatriciana

Preparation time: 0-10 minutes; Cooking time: 15-30 minutes; Serve: 4

Ingredients:

- 200g Pork cheek
- 1 Medium onion
- 400g Peeled tomatoes
- 3 spoons Oil
- 1 Chile
- Salt

Direction:

1. Chop the onion and cut the pork cheek (removing the hard shell). Put everything in the basket, adding the oil.
2. Close the cover, set the air fryer to 3 minutes at 150^0C to brown. Then pour the tomato, pepper, and salt.
3. Cook for an additional 17 minutes, or until desired cooking is achieved.

Nutrition Value (Amount per Serving):

- Calories 321
- Fat 9g
- Carbohydrate 49g
- Sugars 50g
- Protein 14g
- Cholesterol 20mg

Pork Chops with Chicory Treviso

Preparation time: 10-20; Cooking time: 0-15; Serve: 2

Ingredients:

- 4 pork chops
- 40g butter
- Flour to taste
- 1 chicory stalk
- Salt to taste

Direction:

1. Cut the chicory into small pieces. Place the butter and chicory in pieces on the basket of the air fryer previously preheated at 180^0C and brown for 2 min.
2. Add the previously floured and salted pork slices (directly over the chicory), simmer for 6 minutes turning them over after 3 minutes.
3. Remove the slices and place them on a serving plate, covering them with the rest of the red chicory juice collected at the bottom of the basket.

Nutrition Value (Amount per Serving):

- Calories 504
- Fat 33
- Carbohydrates 0g
- Sugars 0g
- Protein 42g
- Cholesterol 130mg

Venetian Liver

Preparation time: 10-20; Cooking time: 15-30; Serve: 6

Ingredients:

- 500g veal liver
- 2 white onions
- 100g of water
- 2 tbsp vinegar
- Salt and pepper to taste

Direction:

1. Chop the onion and put it inside the pan with the water. Set the air fryer to 180^0C and cook for 20 minutes.
2. Add the liver cut into small pieces and vinegar, close the lid, and cook for an additional 10 minutes.
3. Add salt and pepper.

Nutrition Value (Amount per Serving):

- Calories 131
- Fat 14.19 g
- Carbohydrates 16.40 g
- Sugars 5.15 g
- Protein 25.39 g
- Cholesterol 350.41 mg

Vegetable Cane

Preparation time: 10-20 minutes, Cooking time: more than 60 minutes; Serve: 4

Ingredients:

- 2 calf legs
- 4 carrots
- 4 medium potatoes
- 1 clove garlic
- 300ml Broth
- Leave to taste
- Pepper to taste

Direction:

1. Place the ears, garlic, and half of the broth in the greased basket.
2. Set the temperature to 180^0C.
3. Cook the stems for 40 minutes, turning them in the middle of cooking.
4. Add the vegetables in pieces, salt, pepper, pour the rest of the broth and cook for another 50 minutes (time may vary depending on the size of the hocks).
5. Mix the vegetables and the ears 2 to 3 times during cooking.

Nutrition Value (Amount per Serving):

- Calories 7.9
- Fat 0.49g
- Carbohydrate 0.77g
- Sugar 0.49g
- Protein 0.08mg
- Cholesterol 0mg

Milanese Veal Legs

Preparation time: 10-20 minutes, Cooking time: more than 60 minutes; Serve: 4

Ingredients:

- 1kg beef leg
- 1 onion
- 1 glass of white wine
- 150g hot broth
- Taste Flour
- Salt, pepper to taste
- 1 bunch of parsley
- ½ grated lemon
- 1 clove garlic

Direction:

1. Place the chopped onion in the basket. Brown for 4 minutes at 150^0C.
2. Add the lightly floured ears the white wine, season with salt and pepper and simmer for 6 minutes.
3. Turn the spikes, add the broth, and cook for another 50 minutes turning the meat 1-2 times.
4. At this point, add the chopped parsley, a grated peel of half a lemon and a clove of garlic and continue cooking for the remaining 10 minutes.
5. Serve hot with the juice that has formed in the cooking vessel.

Nutrition Value (Amount per Serving):

- Calories 499
- Fat 22.54g
- Carbohydrate 38.25g
- Sugars 2.27g
- Protein 34.23g
- Cholesterol 160mg

Veal, speck, and cheese paupiettes

Preparation time: 10-20 minutes, Cooking time: 15-30 minutes; Serve: 6

Ingredients:

- 12 slices of veal
- 6 speck slices
- 12 slices of provola
- Salt to taste
- Pepper to taste

Direction:

1. Place half a slice of stain and one of provola on each slice of veal; Roll each slice and close them with toothpicks.
2. Pour the oil and place the paupiettes in the basket, season with salt and pepper.
3. Set the air fryer to 180°C.
4. Cook the paupiettes for 15 minutes, turning them around after about 8 to 9 minutes.

Nutrition Value (Amount per Serving):

- Calories 261
- Carbohydrates 0g
- Fat 11g
- Sugar 0g
- Protein 30g
- Cholesterol 0mg

Fried Pork

Preparation time: 10 – 20 minutes, Cooking time: 0 – 15 minutes; Serve: 4

Ingredients:

- 300 g pork loin
- 2 egg yolks
- 4 tsp Worcestershire sauce:
- Salt to taste
- Taste Flour
- Gusto breadcrumbs

Direction:

1. Put the egg yolk, Worcestershire sauce and some flour (to thicken the sauce) in a bowl.
2. Cut the meat into pieces, lightly salt, and then pass it first in the sauce (previously prepared) and in breadcrumbs.
3. Grease the basket of the air fryer.
4. Preheat the air fryer for 1 minute at 200^0C.
5. Add the pork and cook for 10 minutes, turning the meat halfway through cooking.

Nutrition Value (Amount per Serving):

- Calories 178
- Fat 11.89g
- Carbohydrates 0g
- Sugars 0g
- Protein 16.66g
- Cholesterol 51mg

Roast Pork with Vegetables

Preparation time: 10-20 minutes, Cooking time: more than 60 minutes; Serve: 8

Ingredients:

- 1 kg of pork loin
- 4 carrots
- 3 potatoes
- 1 onion
- 1 clove garlic
- 250 ml broth
- Salt and pepper to taste

Direction:

1. Place the tenderloin in the center of the tank, as well as the vegetables in small pieces, salt, pepper and pour a little broth.
2. Set the temperature to 160^0C. Simmer for 1 hour and 30 minutes. Mix the vegetables occasionally and turn the loin halfway through cooking. Add some broth as necessary to keep the meat tender.

Nutrition Value (Amount per Serving):

- Calories 487.3
- Fat 16.7 g
- Carbohydrate 40.3 g
- Sugars 1.1 g
- Protein 44.9 g
- Cholesterol 95.3 mg

Saltimbocca Roman Veal

Preparation time: 10 – 20 minutes, Cooking time: 0 – 15 minutes; Serve: 4

Ingredients:

- 70-80 g See
- 16 slices of raw ham
- 16 sage leaves
- 20 g butter
- Salt to taste
- Pepper to taste

Address:

1. Place the meat slices on a sheet of parchment paper. Arrange the ham slices on the meat, put the washed sage leaf, roll, and close with a toothpick.
2. Place the butter in the basket at 150°C. Melt the butter for 2 min.
3. Add the meat and simmer for 6 minutes.

Nutrition Value (Amount per Serving):

- Calories 323
- Fat 18g
- Carbohydrates 1.7g
- Sugars 0.4g
- Protein 29g
- Cholesterol 124mg

Sautéed Meat with Potatoes

Preparation time: 10-20 minutes, Cooking time: 30-45 minutes; Serve: 6

Ingredients:

- 750g beef
- 350 g of potatoes
- 200 ml of hot broth
- 250 g of tomato coulis
- 1 onion
- Salt to taste
- Pepper to taste

Direction:

1. Chop the onion and put it in the basket previously greased.
2. Set the temperature to 150^0C.
3. Brown the onion for 3 to 4 minutes and then add the pieces of meat, broth, salt, and pepper.
4. Cook the meat for 20 minutes and add the potatoes and the tomato coulis.
5. Cook for another 20 to 25 minutes, mixing the sautéed with a wooden spoon 3 to 4 times during cooking to prevent it from drying out too much.

Nutrition Value (Amount per Serving):

- Calories 317
- Carbohydrates 13g
- Fat 18g
- Sugars 1g
- Protein 24g
- Cholesterol 73mg

Sautéed Pork with Peppers

Preparation time: 10 – 20 minutes, Cooking time: 15 – 30 minutes; Serve: 6

Ingredients:

- 600 g pieces of pork taken from the loin or shoulder
- 200 g of peppers
- 1 shallot
- Salt to taste
- Pepper to taste

Direction:

1. Preheat the air fryer at 150^0C for 5 minutes. Spray the basket.
2. Chop the shallot and cut the peppers into strips Place the shallot and oil in the basket then brown for 2 minutes.
3. Add the peppers and simmer for another 8 minutes.
4. Finally pour the pieces of pork, salt, pepper, and simmer for another 10 minutes.

Nutrition Value (Amount per Serving):

- Calories 334.2
- Fat 11.5 g
- Carbohydrate 31.8 g
- Sugars 2.0 g
- Protein 24.5 g
- Cholesterol 59.2 mg

Chapter 6

Vegan and Vegetarian Recipes

Frying Potatoes

Preparation time: 5 minutes; Cooking time: 40 minutes; Serve: 4

Ingredients:

- 5 to 6 medium potatoes
- Olive oil in a spray bottle if possible
- Mill salt
- Freshly ground pepper

Direction:

1. Wash the potatoes well and dry them.
2. Brush with a little oil on both sides if not with the oil
3. Crush some ground salt and pepper on top.
4. Place the potatoes in the fryer basket
5. Set the cooking at 190°C for 40 minutes, in the middle of cooking turn the potatoes for even cooking on both sides.
6. At the end of cooking, remove the potatoes from the basket, cut them in half and slightly scrape the melting potato inside and add only a little butter, and enjoy!

Nutrition Value (Amount per Serving):

- Calories 365
- Fat 17g
- Carbohydrates 48g
- Sugars 0.3g
- Protein 4g
- Cholesterol 0mg

Avocado Fries

Preparation time: 5 minutes Cooking time: 10 minutes; Serve: 1

Ingredients:

- 1 egg
- 1 ripe avocado
- ½ tsp salt
- ½ cup of panko breadcrumbs

Direction:

1. Preheat the air fryer to 400°F (200°C) for 5 minutes.
2. Remove the avocado pit and cut into fries. In a small bowl, whisk the egg with the salt.
3. Enter the breadcrumbs on a plate.
4. Dip the quarters in the egg mixture, then in the breadcrumbs.
5. Put them in the fryer. Cook for 8-10 minutes.
6. Turn halfway through cooking.

Nutrition Value (Amount per Serving):

- Calories 390
- Fat 32g
- Carbohydrates 24g
- Sugars 3g
- Protein 4g
- Cholesterol 0mg

Crispy French Fries

Preparation time: 5 minutes; Cooking time: 10 minutes; Serve: 2

Ingredients:

- 2 medium sweet potatoes
- 2 tsp olive oil
- ½ tsp salt
- ½ tsp garlic powder
- ¼ tsp paprika
- Black pepper

Direction:

1. Preheat the hot air fryer to 400°F (200°C)
2. Spray the basket with a little oil.
3. Cut the sweet potatoes into potato chips about 1 cm wide.
4. Add oil, salt, garlic powder, pepper and paprika.
5. Cook for 8 minutes, without overloading the basket.
6. Repeat 2 or 3 times, as necessary.

Nutrition Value (Amount per Serving):

- Calories 240
- Fat 9g
- Carbohydrates 36g
- Sugars 1g
- Protein 3g
- Cholesterol 0mg

Frying Potatoes with Butter

Preparation time: 5 minutes; Cooking time: 10 minutes; Serve: 2

Ingredients:

- 2 Russet potatoes
- Butter
- Fresh parsley (optional)

Direction:

1. Spray the basket with a little oil.
2. Open your potatoes along.
3. Make some holes with a fork.
4. Add the butter and parsley.
5. Transfer to the basket. If your air fryer to a temperature of 198°C (390°F).
6. Cook for 30 to 40 minutes.
7. Try about 30 minutes. Bon Appetite!

Nutrition Value (Amount per Serving):

- Calories 365
- Fat 17g
- Carbohydrates 48g
- Sugars 0.3g
- Protein 4g
- Cholesterol 0mg

Homemade French Fries

Preparation time: 5 minutes; Cooking time: 10 minutes; Serve: 2

Ingredients:

- 2.5 lb. sliced and sliced potato chips
- 1 tbsp olive oil
- Salt and pepper to taste
- 1 tsp salt to season or paprika

Direction:

1. Put the fries in a bowl with very cold water.
2. Let it soak for at least 30 minutes.
3. Drain completely. Add the oil. Shake
4. Put them in the fryer bowl. Cook for 15 to 25 minutes. Set to 380°F (193°C).
5. Set the time according to your preferences or the power of your fryer to 23 minutes.

Nutrition Value (Amount per Serving):

- Calories 118
- Fat 7g
- Carbohydrates 27
- Sugars 1g
- Protein 2
- Cholesterol 0mg

Mini pepper/tomato/shallot/goat cheese tartlets

Preparation time: 10 minutes; Cooking time: 15 minutes; Serve: 4-6

Ingredients:

- 1 pure butter puff pastry
- 3 peppers + 2 tomatoes + 1 shallot + 1 degermed garlic clove
- 1 whole egg + 2 tbsp salad seeds (squash, sunflower, sesame ......)
- 3 tablespoons cheese in cubes + ½ goat cheese log + 50 g grated emmental cheese
- 6/8 mini silicone molds (round, square, heart ....)
- Salt + pepper 5 berries

Direction:

1. Put the grid / cubes in the 11 in 1 mandolin and cut all the vegetables (cleaned) into small pieces.
2. Beat the egg in an omelet and add the cut vegetables, the cubed cheese, the seeds, salt, and pepper.
3. Unroll the puff pastry and cut circles (squares of hearts ...) and darken the mini molds. Prick the bottom with a fork.
4. Garnish with the egg/vegetable preparation and add a little goat cheese and grated emmental cheese on top.
5. Place the molds on the fryer grid, close the hood, and program the "15-minute pie" function at 150^0C.
6. When it is well cooked, remove the grid with the tongs. Serve hot or warm with a salad.

Nutrition Value (Amount per Serving):

- Calories 152g
- Fat 9g
- Carbohydrates 10g
- Sugars 10g
- Protein 4g
- Cholesterol 0mg

Almond Apples

Preparation time: 10 minutes; Cooking time: 45 minutes; Serve: 5-6

Ingredients:

- 600 g of peeled potatoes
- 2 egg yolks
- 2 eggs
- 60g of almond powder
- Salt,
- Pepper
- frying oil
- 30g of butter
- 50g of almond chips
- 50g of breadcrumbs
- 50g of flour

Direction:

1. Peel the potatoes (if you feel like it, instead of throwing the husks, baked shell chips, it's a delight).
2. Cut the potatoes into cubes and cook them in salted water (starting with cold water) approximately 15 minutes after boiling.
3. Drain and puree with a potato masher. Add salt and pepper.
4. Add the egg yolks, butter, and almond powder, mix well.
5. Place in the refrigerator for a quarter of an hour, then roll balls into the palm of your hand. Then, roll them rolling successively in flour, beaten eggs in an omelet, then in a mixture of breadcrumbs and flaked almonds.
6. Let cool for 15 minutes.
7. Put them in the air fryer at 180°C for 15 minutes. Then place the almond apples on a paper towel.

Nutrition Value (Amount per Serving):

- Calories 284.0
- Fat 19.1 g
- Carbohydrate 27.9 g
- Sugars 13.8 g
- Protein 5.0 g
- Cholesterol 0.0 mg

French fries without dry

Ingredients:

- 500g of French fries
- 1 tbsp oil

Preparation:

1. Peel and cut the potatoes, using a knife or a "fried cut".
2. Rinse with water and dry the fries.
3. Put them in a bowl and add the oil spoon, mix well.
4. Preheat the air fryer to 160°C. Put the fries in the basket for 15 minutes.
5. Pour the fries in the bowl, mix, and pass the fryer to more than 200°C.
6. Put the fries back in the basket and cook again for about 10 minutes. Look carefully because the overhead comes quickly!

Nutrition Value (Amount per Serving):

- Calories 118
- Sugars 1g
- Fat 7g
- Protein 2
- Carbohydrates 27
- Cholesterol 0mg

Bugnes Lyonnaises

Preparation: 30 minutes; Rest: 2 hours; Cook: 15 minutes

Ingredients:

- 250 g flour
- ½ packet of yeast
- 50g of powdered sugar
- 50g butter
- 2 eggs
- 1 tsp rum
- 1 pinch of salt
- Frying oil

Direction:

1. Soften the butter; beat the eggs with a fork.
2. Place the flour in a bowl; add the salt, the butter, the beaten eggs, the aroma.
3. Mix until you have a consistent paste. Form a ball and let stand at least 2 hours in the fridge.
4. Heat the fryer oil at 150^0C for 15 minutes.
5. Stretch the dough to a thickness of 5 mm. Cut into strips of 10 cm by 4 cm and make an incision in the center of 5 cm.
6. Pass a corner of the strip in the incision to tie a knot or leave it as is.
7. Dip the bugnes in the fryer, flip them 1 time and drain once cooked on absorbent paper.
8. Sprinkle with icing sugar or icing sugar and serve hot.

Nutrition Value (Amount per Serving):

- Calories 140
- Carbohydrate 6 g
- Fat 13 g
- Protein 1 g
- Sodium 29 mg
- Sugar 1 g

Green salad with roasted pepper

Preparation time: 5 minutes; Cooking time: 10 minutes; Serve: 2

Ingredients:

- 1 red pepper
- 1 tbsp lemon juice
- 3 tbsp yogurt
- 2 tbsp olive oil
- Freshly ground black pepper
- 1 romaine lettuce, cut into large strips
- 50g arugula leaves

Direction:

1. Preheat the Air Fryer to 200°C.
2. Place the pepper in the basket and insert it into the Air Fryer. Set the timer for 10 minutes and roast the pepper until the skin is slightly burned.
3. Then cut the pepper into quarters and remove the seeds and skin. Cut the pepper into strips.
4. Prepare vinaigrette in a bowl with 2 tablespoons of pepper juice, lemon juice, yogurt, and olive oil. Add pepper and salt according to your taste.
5. Mix the lettuce and arugula leaves in the vinaigrette and garnish the salad with the pepper strips.

Nutrition Value (Amount per Serving):

- Calories 47.3
- Fat 0.4 g
- Carbohydrate 10.8 g
- Sugars 2.0 g
- Protein 1.8 g
- Cholesterol 0.0 mg

Fat Free Crispy Fries

Preparation time: about 15 minutes; Cook time: 10 to 35 minutes; Serve: 4

Ingredients:

- 500g of special fries
- 1 tbsp olive oil
- 1 freezer bag
- Salt + pepper

Direction:

1. Peel the potatoes, cut them with a potato chip cutter, rinse them with clean water and dry them well with a cloth.
2. It is important to cut all the potatoes evenly; otherwise you may have some overcooked and not enough fries.
3. Place the sliced fries in a freezer bag, add 1 tablespoon of oil, close the bag, and stir everything.
4. Place the French fries in the basket, close it, and close the lid of the fryer and set to 230°C to 35 minutes.
5. At the end of cooking, remove the basket with the tongs and remove the fries. Add salt and pepper.

Nutrition Value (Amount per Serving):

- Calories 118
- Fat 7g
- Carbohydrates 27
- Sugars 1g
- Protein 2
- Cholesterol 0mg

Marinated Potatoes with Chimichurri Sauce

Preparation time: 20 minutes; Cooking time: 45 minutes; Serve: 4

Ingredients:

- 1kg to 1.2kg of potatoes
- 2 tablespoons chimichurri sauce

Direction:

1. Depending on the taste, you can peel the potatoes, but the real potatoes are prepared with the skin.
2. Wash the potatoes before cutting them.
3. Cut them in quarters to get the shape of the potatoes and place them in a freezer bag.
4. Add the sauce and use the solid closure of the sachet to keep it closed.
5. Mix everything by handling the bag in all directions. Potatoes should be well impregnated with the preparation.
6. Pour all the preparation in the air fryer without oil.
7. Set the air fryer at 180^0C for 45 minutes and serve immediately after the end of cooking.

Nutrition Value (Amount per Serving):

- Calories 367
- Sugars 2.0 g
- Fat 18.4 g
- Protein 5.7 g
- Carbohydrate 45 g
- Cholesterol 0mg

Homemade Gluten Free Spicy Chips

Preparation time: 25 minutes; Cooking time: 30 minutes; Serve: 1

Ingredients:

- 500g of potatoes to choose from among those with firm meat
- 1 tbsp vegetable oil
- 1 pinch of salt
- 1 mixture of texmex spices

Direction:

1. Peel the potatoes and cut them into slices approximately 2 millimeters thick. Preferably use a mandolin for a very fine and regular cut.
2. Rinse the potatoes to get rid of their starch and let them stand for 15 minutes in a bowl of cold water.
3. Drain the potatoes and dry them with a paper towel by simply sliding them. Avoid rubbing them as they could break.
4. Pour the potatoes in the fryer and cover them with the necessary tablespoon of oil.
5. Set the air fryer at 150^0C for 30 minutes.
6. Be sure to stir the fries with a wooden utensil every ten minutes to make sure they cook perfectly.
7. Wait 5 minutes before the end of cooking to add salt and spices.

Nutrition Value (Amount per Serving):

- Calories 150
- Cal
- 17%
- Carbohydrates 15g
- Fat 32g
- Protein 1g
- Sugars 3g
- Cholesterol 0mg

Funghetto Eggplant (Golden Neapolitan)

Preparation time: 0-10 minutes; Cooking time: 15-30 minutes; Serve:

Ingredients:

- 600g Eggplant
- 100g Broth
- 1 Garlic clove
- Salt
- Pepper
- 3 spoons Olive oil
- Parsley

Direction:

1. Wash the eggplants, dry them, and cut them into 1.5 cm cubes.
2. Place the mixing blade in the tank
3. Pour oil and peeled garlic, close the lid.
4. Set the air fryer to 150^0C to brown for about 2 min.
5. Add eggplant, broth, salt and pepper and simmer for another 23 min.
6. Finally, before serving, sprinkle with chopped fresh parsley.

Nutrition Value (Amount per Serving):

- Calories 142
- Fat 12.9g
- Carbohydrate 5.20g
- Protein 1.9g
- Sugars 0g
- Cholesterol 0.1mg

Fried Bananas

Preparation time: 0-10 minutes; Cooking time: 0 – 15 minutes; Serve: 3

Ingredients:

- 3 Bananas
- 2 Eggs
- Breadcrumbs
- Flour at discretion
- Salt
- 1 tsp Oil

Direction:

1. Peel the bananas and cut them into sections of approximately 2 to 3 cm.
2. Pass them first in the flour, then in the egg beaten with salt and then in the breadcrumbs.
3. Heat the air fryer at 180^0C for 10 minutes. Then, place the breaded bananas.
4. Cook the bananas for 8 to 10 minutes, turning them 2 to 3 times during cooking to match the Dorado.
5. Serve warm.

Nutrition Value (Amount per Serving):

- Calories 262.4
- Fat 12.1 g
- Carbohydrate 33.9 g
- Sugars 20.7 g
- Protein 1.3 g
- Cholesterol 30.5 mg

Sautéed air mushrooms and parsley

Preparation time: 10 – 20 minutes; Cooking time: 15 – 30 minutes; Serve: 6

Ingredients:

- 600 g mushrooms
- 1 clove garlic
- 1 tsp olive oil
- Parsley
- Leave at discretion
- Black pepper at discretion

Direction:

1. Clean the mushrooms well and chop them.
2. Place the garlic and oil inside the basket close. Set the temperature to 150°C.
3. Brown for 2 minutes.
4. Add the mushrooms and cook for another 15 minutes.
5. Add (at discretion) salt and pepper, parsley, and finish cooking for another 3 minutes.

Nutrition Value (Amount per Serving):

- Calories 130
- Fat 7g
- Carbohydrates 17g
- Sugars 4g
- Protein 4g
- Cholesterol 0mg

Cauliflowers au gratin

Preparation time: 20-30 minutes; Cooking time: 15-30 minutes; Serve: 6

Ingredients:

- 800g cauliflower
- 4 slices of cheese
- ½ liter of Béchamel
- Parmesan to taste

Direction:

1. Separately, cook the cauliflowers in water. Meanwhile, prepare ½ liter of bechamel (dose: 500 ml of milk, 50 g of flour, 50 g of butter, salt, and nutmeg).

2. Pour some bechamel into the basket. Arrange the cauliflower flowers, covered with the slices of cheese and cover with the béchamel sauce. Sprinkle with Parmesan cheese.

3. Set the air fryer to 150^0C. Simmer for about 20 minutes or according to the degree of gratin desired.

Nutrition Value (Amount per Serving):

- Calories 285
- Fat 19g
- Carbohydrates 17g
- Sugars 2.5g
- Protein 14g
- Cholesterol 55mg

Peach Clafoutis

Preparation time: 20 – 30 minutes; Cooking time: 30 – 45 minutes; Serve: 10

Ingredients:

- 300 g flour
- 150g butter
- 150g of sugar
- 4 eggs
- 1 sachet of baking powder
- 500g peaches in syrup
- 1 lemon
- 3-4 tbsp milk
- Icing sugar at discretion

Direction:

1. Melt the butter in the microwave; Work the butter, sugar, and eggs in a bowl.
2. Add flour, baking powder, grated lemon peel and milk. Work everything with an electric mixer until you get a smooth and homogeneous mixture.
3. Butter and flour the tank and pour the mixture inside, smearing well.
4. Place a whole peach in the center and place the others (cut into quarters) next to each other following the circumference of the mold.
5. Set the air fryer on the lower heating temperature.
6. Bake the cake for 45 minutes.
7. Let cool and remove it from the tank; sprinkle with icing sugar.

Nutrition Value (Amount per Serving):

- Calories 148
- Carbohydrates 14g
- Fat 8g
- Sugars 6 g
- Protein 4g
- Cholesterol 102mg

Zucchini thinly sliced

Preparation time: 0-10 minutes; Cooking time: 15-30 minutes; Serve: 6

Ingredients:

- 600g zucchini
- 1 clove garlic
- 100 ml of water
- 1 tsp olive oil
- Parsley Taste
- Salt to taste
- Pepper to taste

Direction:

1. Wash and turn the zucchini, then dry them and cut them into rings. Add the oil and peeled garlic to the basket.
2. Set the temperature to 150^0C.
3. Brown for about 2 minutes, then remove the garlic from the tank and pour the zucchini with the water, season with salt and pepper and close the lid.
4. Simmer for 23 minutes. At the end of cooking, add the chopped parsley, a drizzle of oil and serve.

Nutrition Value (Amount per Serving):

- Calories 21
- Fat 0.2g
- Carbohydrates 3.9g
- Sugars 3.1g
- Protein 1.5g
- Cholesterol 0mg

Couscous with Vegetables

Preparation time: 10-20 minutes; Cooking time: 30-45 minutes; Serve: 8

Ingredients:

- 50g carrot
- Eggplant 250g
- 50g cherry tomatoes
- 1 shallot
- 150g broth
- 250g zucchini
- Salt to taste
- 1 clove garlic
- Chili pepper
- 375g couscous
- 400 ml of water
- Butter taste
- 1 ml of olive oil

Direction:

1. Peel the garlic, cut the chili into pieces, chop the shallot and place everything on the baking sheet, distributing it well through the bottom; add the oil. Before you start cooking, wash, and cut eggplants, zucchini, carrots, and small diced tomatoes (the latter should be reserved as they will be added to couscous when they are cold).

2. Set the air fryer to 150^0C and brown for 3 minutes. Add carrots, broth, and simmer for another 6 min. Finally pour the eggplant and zucchini, salt and pepper and simmer for another 25 minutes.

3. In addition to preparing the semolina by putting the water in a saucepan, boil, pour a small spoonful of salt. Add the couscous in the rain, oil, mix and stop the fire. Let swell for 3 min. Add a pinch of butter and cook again for another 3 min. mixing regularly with a fork to shell properly.

4. As soon as the vegetables have cooled, add the small tomatoes, and pour everything into a bowl with the couscous.

Nutrition Value (Amount per Serving):

- Calories 219.6
- Fat 4.0 g
- Carbohydrate 40.3 g
- Sugars 0.0 g
- Protein 6.5 g
- Cholesterol 0.0 mg

Rillette mushroom crusts

Preparation time: more than 30, Cooking time: 15 - 30, Calories: 273

Ingredients:

- 400g mushrooms
- 1 shallot
- 40g nuts without shell
- 150g of butter
- Parsley at discretion
- 1 tsp olive oil
- Bread slices

Direction:

1. Cut the shallot finely and pour it into the greased basket previously preheat at 150^0C for 5 minutes.
2. Let brown for 2 minutes.
3. Add sliced mushrooms, salt, and cook for 20 minutes.
4. At the end of cooking, mix the mushrooms, soft butter and nuts until a homogeneous mixture is obtained.
5. Put everything in the fridge for 1 hour.
6. Remove the preparation paddle from the basket (be careful, it will be hot), place the slices of bread inside and toast them for 4 to 5 minutes or until golden brown.
7. Fill each crouton with the rillette.

Nutrition Value (Amount per Serving):

- Calories 190
- Fat 1.5g
- Carbohydrates 36g
- Sugars 3g
- Protein 7g
- Cholesterol 0mg

Mediterranean Bream

Preparation time: 10-20 minutes; Cooking time: 15-30 minutes; Serve: 2

Ingredients:

- 2 gold
- 200g cherry tomatoes
- 100g of black olives
- 1 clove garlic
- Thyme to taste
- Leaves to taste
- Pepper to taste
- 1 tsp peanut oil

Direction:

1. First, remove the golden scales. Clean them and gut them. Salt and pepper inside the belly, add a clove of garlic and two sprigs of thyme.
2. Grease the basket with the oil.
3. Cut the tomatoes in half and add them to the basket with the black olives and capers; salt everything
4. Set the temperature to 150°C and cook for 25 minutes.

Nutrition Value (Amount per Serving):

- Calories 248
- Carbohydrates 22g
- Fat 12g
- Sugars 3g
- Protein 8g
- Cholesterol 0mg

Draniki

Preparation time: 10-20 minutes; Cooking time: 15-30 minutes; Serve: 2

Ingredients:

- 4 medium potatoes
- ½ onion
- 1 carrot
- 1 egg
- 100g flour
- Leaves to taste
- 1 tsp oil

Direction:

1. Peel the potatoes, the onion and the carrot and wash them well.
2. Using a food processor cut all vegetables in julienne and place them in a large bowl.
3. Add the egg, salt, and flour (the doses of the latter may vary depending on the degree of moisture present in the vegetables) and mix well.
4. Cover the bottom of the basket with baking paper and pour a little of the mixture with a tablespoon and spread well.
5. Fill the useful space inside the tank (about 5 to 6 empanadas at a time).
6. Set the air fryer to 180^0C.
7. Cook for 10 to 12 minutes depending on the degree of browning desired.
8. After finishing the mixture, remove the baking paper, grease the bottom of the tank, and brown the previously cooked empanadas for another 2 minutes on each side.

Nutrition Value (Amount per Serving):

- Calories 84
- Carbohydrates 16g
- Fat 2g
- Sugars 0g
- Protein 3g
- Cholesterol 0mg

Chips

Preparation time: 10-20 minutes; Cooking time: 30-45 minutes; Serve: 8

Ingredients:

- 1500g of fresh potatoes
- 1 tsp peanut oil
- Fine salt to taste

Direction:

1. Peel the potatoes and cut them into sticks of approximately 1 cm per side.
2. Put the cut potatoes in water for a few minutes and rinse thoroughly.
3. Drain and clean well with a paper towel.
4. Pour the potatoes and the correct amount of oil in the pan.
5. Cook for 37/40 minutes at 180^0C. Salt then serve.

Nutrition Value (Amount per Serving):

- Calories 365
- Sugars 0.3g
- Fat 17g
- Protein 4g
- Carbohydrates 48g
- Cholesterol 0mg

French Fries with Paprika

Preparation time: 10-20 minutes, Cooking time: 15-30 minutes; Serve: 8

Ingredients:

- 700g of carrots
- 1 tsp sweet paprika
- 1 tsp oil

Direction:

1. Peel the carrots and cut them into sticks.
2. Add carrots and paprika in the basket. Set the temperature to 180^0C.
3. Cook the carrots for about 20 minutes (time may vary depending on the size of the carrots).

Nutrition Value (Amount per Serving):

- Calories 299
- Carbohydrates 33g
- Sugars 3g
- Fat 16g
- Protein 7g
- Cholesterol 163 mg

Frozen French Fries

Cooking time: 15-30 minutes; Serve: 8

Ingredients:

- 1000g Standard French fries (10 X 10) mm frozen
- Fine salt to taste

Direction:

1. Preheat the air fryer at 150^0C.
2. Let cook for 27 minutes: salt and serve.

Nutrition Value (Amount per Serving):

- Calories 150.0
- Fat 0.0 g
- Carbohydrate 20.0 g
- Sugars 0.0 g
- Protein 2.0 g
- Cholesterol 0.0 mg

Beans in sauce

Preparation time: 0-10 minutes, Cooking time: 15-30 minutes; Serve: 8

Ingredients:

- 500g canned beans
- 300g of tomato puree
- ½ carrot
- 1 onion
- ½ sprig of rosemary
- Salt and pepper to taste
- 1 tsp olive oil

Direction:

1. Prepare a chopped carrot and onion and place it inside the cooking tray with rosemary. Grease the basket with the oil.
2. Set the air fryer to 150°C and brown for 4 min.
3. Add the drained beans from your vegetable water and rinse thoroughly, simmer for another 3 min.
4. Add the tomato, ½ glass of water, salt and pepper and continue cooking for another 13 minutes.

Nutrition Value (Amount per Serving):

- Calories 270
- Fat 1g
- Carbohydrates 53g
- Sugars 14g
- Protein 14g
- Cholesterol 0mg

Spicy Potatoes

Preparation time: 10-20 minutes; Cooking time: 30-45 minutes; Serve: 8

Ingredients:

- 1250g of fresh potatoes
- 10g sweet paprika
- Tomato puree
- 2 tbsp vinegar
- Salt and pepper to taste

Direction:

1. Peel the potatoes and cut them into 1 cm cubes on each side. Put the potatoes in the water for a few minutes and rinse them well. Drain and clean with a paper towel.
2. Pour the potatoes, rosemary, and the exact amount of oil inside the tank, salt, and pepper.
3. Set the air fryer to 160^0C and cook for 25 min.
4. Add the paprika, tomato puree and vinegar, then finish cooking and simmer for another 10 minutes.
5. Prepare the "tapas" by piercing the potatoes with toothpicks.

Nutrition Value (Amount per Serving):

- Calories 250
- Carbohydrates 33g
- Fat 11g
- Sugars 0g
- Protein 4g
- Cholesterol 0mg

Frozen Potatoes

Cooking time: 15-30 minutes; Serve: 8

Ingredients:

- 1000 g of potatoes in frozen rooms
- Fine salt to taste

Direction:

1. Cook for 30 minutes at 160^0C.
2. Salt and serve

Nutrition Value (Amount per Serving):

- Calories 18.2
- Fat 0.0g
- Carbohydrate 4.1g
- Protein 0.6g
- Cholesterol 0mg

Potatoes (Unpeeled) And Yogurt Sauce

Preparation time: 10 – 20 minutes, Cooking time: 30 – 45 minutes; Serve: 4

Ingredients:

- 750 g of fresh potatoes
- 1 pepper
- 1 onion
- Salt taste
- Basil at ease
- 50 g lean yogurt
- 50 g of mayonnaise
- 20 g tomato sauce
- 1 pinch sweet paprika

Direction:

1. Wash the potatoes and let them soak in cold water and baking soda for 15 minutes and then brush them well with water.
2. Cut them in quarters and put them in the basket previously greased.
3. Set the air fryer to 150^0C.
4. Cook the potatoes for 15 minutes and then add the chopped pepper and sliced onion; Salt.
5. Cook for another 15 minutes and then add the fresh basil cut from the menu.
6. Cook for another 15 minutes.
7. If you want to accompany the potatoes with the yogurt sauce, simply mix all the ingredients until you get a creamy sauce.

Nutrition Value (Amount per Serving):

- Calories 49.1
- Fat 2.5 g
- Carbohydrate 2.4 g
- Sugars 1.7 g
- Protein 4.1 g
- Cholesterol 5.2 mg

Frozen New Potatoes

Cooking time: 30-45 minutes; Serve: 8

Ingredients:

- 1200 g of frozen new potatoes
- Fine salt to taste

Direction:

1. Pour the potatoes in the basket.
2. Cook for 38 minutes at 180^0C.
3. Salt and serve.

Nutrition Value (Amount per Serving):

- Calories 89
- Carbohydrates 19g
- Fat 0g
- Sugars 0g
- Protein 2g
- Cholesterol 0mg

Potatoes, Beets and Carrots

Preparation time: 10-20 minutes, Cooking time: 30-45 minutes; Serve: 6

Ingredients:

- 300g beet
- 300 g of carrots
- 300 g of potatoes
- 2 cloves of garlic
- Rosemary to taste
- Salt to taste
- Pepper to taste

Direction:

1. Clean, wash all vegetables (beets, carrots, and potatoes) and cut them into pieces of 2 to 3 cm.
2. Put the garlic clove, chopped vegetables, rosemary and spray the basket; Season with salt and pepper.
3. Cook for about 35 minutes at 150^0C.

Nutrition Value (Amount per Serving):

- Calories 170.5
- Fat 7.1 g
- Carbohydrate 26.5 g
- Sugars 9.5 g
- Protein 3.4 g
- Cholesterol 0.0 mg

Frozen Onion Rings

Cooking time: 15-30 minutes; Serve: 6

Ingredients:

- 15 pieces onion rings: 15 pieces
- Fine salt to taste

Direction:

3. Cook everything for 15 minutes at 180^0C.

Nutrition Value (Amount per Serving):

- Calories 220
- Sugar 5g
- Fat 11g
- Protein 4g
- Carbohydrates 27g
- Cholesterol 0mg

Sautéed Potatoes and Pumpkin

Preparation time: 10 – 20 minutes, Cooking time: 15 – 30 minutes; Serve: 4

Ingredients:

- 450 g of potatoes
- 550 g pumpkin
- 20 g of breadcrumbs
- Coarse salt

Direction:

1. Preheat the air fryer to 180^0C for 5 minutes.
2. Thoroughly clean the pumpkin and potatoes and cut them into large pieces. Pour all ingredients into the basket.
3. Cook for 30 minutes or until you get the crispy you want.

Nutrition Value (Amount per Serving):

- Calories 30
- Fat 0.1g
- Carbohydrates 8g
- Sugars 3.2g
- Protein 1.2g
- Cholesterol 0mg

Rice spaghetti with vegetables

Preparation time: 10 – 20 minutes; Cooking time: 15 – 30 minutes; Serve: 4

Ingredients:

- 100 g of celery
- 150 g of carrots
- 150g kale
- 2 scallions
- 2 tbsp soy sauce
- 100 g of bean sprouts
- 200 g of rice spaghetti

Direction:

1. Spray the basket of the air fryer. Cut all the vegetables in julienne and put the celery, chives, and carrots in the basket.
2. Set the air fryer to 150⁰C. Cook for 10 minutes.
3. Add the sprouts and soy sauce and cook for another 10 minutes.
4. Meanwhile, cook the rice spaghetti in salted water and boil and serve with the previously prepared sauce.

Nutrition Value (Amount per Serving):

- Calories 235.0
- Fat 10.9 g
- Carbohydrate 34.7 g
- Sugars 6.4 g
- Protein 13.9 g
- Cholesterol 0.5 mg

Strapatsada

Preparation time: 10-20 minutes; Cooking time: 15-30 minutes; Serve: 4

Ingredients:

- ½ onion
- 1 red pepper
- 100g mushrooms
- 300 g of tomatoes
- 6 eggs
- Fine salt to taste
- Black pepper to taste

Direction:

1. Cut the mushrooms (washed) and onions in julienne.
2. Distribute everything in the tank with the oil.
3. Set the temperature to 180^{0}C and Cook for 12 minutes.
4. Add the tomatoes (skinless) cut into pieces, salt, and cook for another 8 minutes.
5. Remove the trowel (take care that it is hot!) And distribute the vegetables at the basket.
6. In a bowl, beat the eggs with salt and pepper and pour all over the vegetables. Cook another 7 to 8 minutes.

Nutrition Value (Amount per Serving):

- Calories 380
- Carbohydrates
- Fat 30g
- Sugars 6g
- Protein 19g
- Cholesterol 370g

Chicory Strudel

Preparation time: 10-20 minutes; Cooking time: 30-45 minutes; Serve: 6

Ingredients:

- 1 puff pastry
- Red chicory
- 100 g of stravecchio cheese
- 100 g of cow mozzarella
- 3 slices of Italian stuffed piglet

Direction:

1. Unroll the puff pastry, cover with a layer of cheese shavings, add the pieces of raw chicory and diced mozzarella.
2. Cover the whole with slices of stuffed piglet and close the puff pastry to form a stake.
3. Place the lining on the baking paper inside the basket.
4. Set the temperature to 160^0C and cook for 35 minutes.
5. Very good with cheese sauce.

Nutrition Value (Amount per Serving):

- Calories 210
- Carbohydrates 30g
- Fat 5g
- Sugars 10g
- Protein 9g
- Cholesterol 0mg

Toast with Eggplant Caviar

Preparation time: 10-20 minutes, Cooking time: 15-30 minutes; Serve: 8

Ingredients:

- Eggplants 450g
- 1 tbsp concentrated tomatoes
- 100 g almonds
- 1 shallot
- 25 g of Parmesan
- 15 basil leaves
- Bread slices

Direction:

1. Cut the shallot finely and pour it into the basket previously greased with the spray.
2. Brown for 2 minutes at $160^0 C$.
3. Add chopped eggplants, tomato puree diluted in 100 ml of water, salt and cook for 23 minutes.
4. Chill the eggplants after cooking. Place the almonds in the basket and roast them for 4 to 5 minutes.
5. Mix eggplant with almonds, parmesan, and basil separately until a homogeneous compound is obtained.
6. Remove the preparation paddle from the tank (be careful, it will be hot), place the slices of bread inside and roast them for 4 to 5 minutes or until golden brown.
7. Fill each crust with the previously prepared sauce.

Nutrition Value (Amount per Serving):

- Calories 91.8
- Fat 6.1 g
- Carbohydrate 9.2 g
- Sugars 0.0 g
- Protein 1.5 g
- Cholesterol 1.3 mg

Provencal Tomatoes

Preparation time: 10 – 20 minutes, Cooking time: 15 – 30 minutes; Serve: 4

Ingredients:

- 4 tomatoes
- 80 g of breadcrumbs
- 1 clove garlic
- 2 marjoram branches
- 1 rosemary branch
- Parsley chopped to taste
- Salt to taste
- Butter to taste

Direction:

1. Remove the top of the tomatoes and drain them. Separately, place all other ingredients (except butter) in a bowl and mix them; The mixture must be quite sandy.
2. Fill the tomatoes and then place them in the basket by adding the butter.
3. Set the temperature to 160^0C and cook for 20 minutes depending on the size of the tomatoes.
4. It can be served both cold and hot.

Nutrition Value (Amount per Serving):

- Calories 69
- Carbohydrates 8g
- Fat 2g
- Sugars 2g
- Protein 3g
- Cholesterol 7g

Potato Omelet

Preparation time: 10 – 20 minutes, Cooking time: 15 – 30 minutes; Serve: 6

Ingredients:

- 600 g of potatoes
- ½ onion
- 6 eggs
- Salt, pepper to taste

Direction:

1. Peel the potatoes and cut them into squares of approximately 1 cm; Peel the onion and cut it into slices that are not very thin.
2. Pour the onion, oil and potatoes in the basket Cook for 25 minutes at 160^0C.
3. Distribute potatoes and onion well in the bottom of the basket. Then pour the previously made egg, salt, and pepper mixture. Continue cooking for another 5 minutes.

Nutrition Value (Amount per Serving):

- Calories 193
- Carbohydrates 27g
- Fat 5g
- Sugars 1g
- Protein 10g
- Cholesterol 185 mg

Vol Au Vent with Mushrooms

Preparation time: 10 - 20 minutes, Cooking time: 15 – 30 minutes; Serve: 6

Ingredients:

- 1 roll of puff pastry
- Whole milk to taste
- 100 g of air sautéed mushrooms and parsley
- Brie to taste

Direction:

1. Unroll the puff pastry, prick the bottom with a fork and cut 18 discs about 7 cm in diameter. Place 6 discs in the bowl covered with baking paper.
2. Make a hole of approximately 3 cm in the other 12 discs and place them two at a time in the large discs. Brush with milk so that they adhere well to each other.
3. Set the temperature to 160^0C
4. Cook for 15 to 17 minutes. Rotate the baking paper after 10 minutes for best results.
5. Fill the vol au vent with a preparation of mushrooms sautéed in air and parsley and cover with a piece of cheese.
6. Serve still hot

Nutrition Value (Amount per Serving):

- Calories 94
- Fat 6.4g
- Carbohydrates 6.7g
- Protein 1.7g

Spanish Potatoes

Preparation time: 10 minutes; Cooking time: 57 minutes; Serve: 2

Ingredients:

- 400 g potato
- Water
- 1 tbsp olive oil
- Salt

Direction:

1. Peel and cut the potato in julienne about 0.5 CM thick.
2. Prepare a bowl with very cold water, if necessary, add ice. Place the cut potatoes for at least 30 minutes to make them starch.
3. Dry each potato with an absorbent napkin and place in another dry bowl.
4. When they are all dry, sprinkle with oil or brush with olive oil and season with salt and whatever you like (sweet paprika, oregano, etc.).
5. In this case place in a fryer without oil at temperature 160^0C for 17 minutes.
6. Set the fryer at 180^0C another 10 minutes and that's it.

Nutrition Value (Amount per Serving):

- Calories 77
- Fat 0.09g
- Carbohydrate 17.47g
- Sugars 0.78g
- Protein 2.02g
- Cholesterol 0mg

Green Salad with Roasted Pepper

Preparation time: 15 minutes; Cooking time: 10 minutes; Serve: 4

Ingredients:

- 1 red pepper
- 1 tbsp lemon juice
- 3 tbsp yogurt
- 2 tbsp olive oil
- Freshly ground black pepper
- 1 romaine lettuce in wide strips
- 50 g arugula leaves

Direction:

1. Preheat the air fryer to 200°C.
2. Place the pepper in the basket and place it in the air fryer. Set the timer to 10 minutes and roast the pepper until the skin is slightly burned.
3. Place the pepper in a bowl and cover it with a lid or with transparent film. Let stand 10 to 15 minutes.
4. Next, cut the pepper into four parts and remove the seeds and skin. Cut the pepper into strips.
5. Mix a dressing in a bowl with 2 tablespoons of the pepper juice, lemon juice, yogurt, and olive oil. Add pepper and salt to taste.
6. Pour the lettuce and arugula leaves into the dressing and garnish the salad with the pepper strips.

Nutrition Value (Amount per Serving):

- Calories 77.9
- Fat 0.4 g
- Carbohydrate 19.3 g
- Sugars 4.6 g
- Protein 2.7 g
- Cholesterol 0.0 mg

Garlic Mushrooms

Preparation time: 10 minutes; Cooking time: 10 minutes; Serve: 2

Ingredients:

- 1 slice of white bread
- 1 crushed garlic clove
- 1 tbsp chopped parsley
- Freshly ground black pepper
- 1 tbsp olive oil
- 12 mushrooms

Direction:

1. Preheat the air fryer to 200°C.
2. Grate the slice of bread until it is thin in the kitchen robot and mix it with the garlic, parsley, and season to taste. Finally, pour the olive oil.
3. Remove the mushroom stems and fill the caps with the breadcrumbs.
4. Place the mushrooms in the basket and place it in the air fryer. Set the timer to 10 minutes. Bake until golden brown and crispy.
5. Serve them on a tray.

Nutrition Value (Amount per Serving):

- Calories 139
- Fat 11.6g
- Carbohydrates 6.1g
- Sugars 3.5g
- Protein 4.7g
- Cholesterol 30.4mg

Roasted Potatoes with Paprika and Greek Yogurt

Preparation time: 10 minutes; Cooking time: 20 minutes; Serve: 4

Ingredients:

- 800 g of white potatoes
- 2 tbsp olive oil
- 1 tbsp spicy paprika
- Freshly ground black pepper
- 150 ml Greek yogurt

Direction:

1. Preheat the air fryer to 180°C. Peel the potatoes and cut them into cubes of 3 cm. Dip the cubes in water for at least 30 minutes. Dry them well with paper towels.
2. In a medium-sized bowl, mix 1 tablespoon of olive oil with the paprika and add pepper to taste. Coat the potato dice with the spiced oil.
3. Place the potato dice in the fryer basket and place it in the air fryer. Set the timer to 20 minutes and fry the dice until golden brown and ready to take. Spin them occasionally.
4. In a small bowl, mix the Greek yogurt with the remaining tablespoon of olive oil and add salt and pepper to taste. Spread the paprika over the mixture. Serve the yogurt as a sauce with the potatoes.
5. Serve the potato dice on a tray and salt them. They will be delicious with ribs or kebabs.

Nutrition Value (Amount per Serving):

- Calories 225.1
- Fat 13.8 g
- Carbohydrate 24.2 g
- Sugars 9.7 g
- Protein 2.5 g
- Cholesterol 0.0 mg

Mini peppers with Goat Cheese

Preparation time: 10 minutes; Cooking time: 8 minutes; Serve: 4

Ingredients:

- 8 mini peppers
- ½ tbsp olive oil
- ½ tbsp dried Italian herbs
- 1 tsp freshly ground black pepper
- 100 g soft goat cheese in eight portions

Direction:

1. Preheat the air fryer to 200°C.
2. Cut the top of the mini peppers and remove the seeds and the membrane.
3. Mix the olive oil in a deep dish with the Italian herbs and pepper. Pour the portions of goat cheese in the oil.
4. Press a serving of goat cheese against each mini pepper and place the mini peppers in the basket next to each other. Insert the basket in the air fryer and set the timer to 8 minutes. Bake the mini peppers until the cheese is melted.
5. Serve mini peppers in small dishes such as snacks or snacks.

Nutrition Value (Amount per Serving):

- Calories 17
- Fat 1g
- Carbohydrates 1g
- Sugar 1g
- Protein 0g
- Cholesterol 60mg

Chapter 7

Desserts

Cake with cream and strawberries

Preparation time: 10 minutes; Cooking time: 15 minutes; Serve: 2

Ingredients:

- 1 pure butter puff pastry to stretch
- 500g strawberries (clean and without skin)
- 1 bowl of custard
- 3 tbsp icing sugar baked at 210°C in the air fryer

Direction:

1. Unroll the puff pastry and place it on the baking sheet. Prick the bottom with a fork and spread the custard. Arrange the strawberries in a circle and sprinkle with icing sugar.
2. Cook in a fryer setting a 210°C for 15 minutes.
3. Remove the cake from the fryer with the tongs and let cool.
4. When serving sprinkle with icing sugar
5. And why not, add some whipped cream.

Nutrition Value (Amount per Serving):

- Calories 212.6
- Fat 8.3 g
- Carbohydrate 31.9 g
- Sugars 17.4 g
- Protein 2.3 g
- Cholesterol 21.4 mg

Caramelized Pineapple and Vanilla Ice Cream

Preparation time: 0-10; Cooking time: 15-30; Serve: 4 people

Ingredients:

- 4 slices Pineapple
- 20g Butter
- 50g Cane sugar
- Ice cream/vanilla cream

Direction:

1. Heat the Air Fryer at 150⁰C for 5 minutes. Let it brown for 15-30 minutes. Then, take it out and top with the cream.

Nutrition Value (Amount per Serving):

- Calories 648
- Fat 36.4g
- Carbohydrates 73.2g
- Sugar 61.6g
- Protein 9.5g
- Cholesterol 94mg

Apple Pie

Preparation time: 20-30; Cooking time: 45-60; Serve: 3

Ingredients:

- 600g Flour
- 350g Margarine
- 150g Sugar
- 2 Eggs
- 50g Breadcrumbs
- 3 Apples
- 75g Raisins
- 75g Sugar
- 1tsp Cinnamon

Direction:

2. Put the flour, sugar, eggs, and margarine nuts in the blender just outside the refrigerator.
3. Mix everything until you get a compact and quite flexible mixture. Let it rest in the refrigerator for at least 30 minutes.
4. Preheat the air fryer at 150^0C for 5 minutes.
5. Spread 2/3 of the mass of broken dough in 3-4 mm thick covering the previously floured and floured tank and making the edges adhere well, which should be at least 2 cm.
6. Place the breadcrumbs, apple slices, sugar, raisins, and cinnamon in the bottom; cover everything with the remaining dough and make holes in the top to allow steam to escape.
7. Cook for 40 minutes and then turn off the lower resistance.
8. Cook for another 20 minutes only with the upper resistance on. Once it has cooled, put it on a plate and serve.

Nutrition Value (Amount per Serving):

- Calories 411
- Fat 19.38g
- Total Carbohydrate 57.5g
- Sugars 50g
- Protein 3.72g
- Cholesterol 0mg

Apple Rotation

Preparation time: 10 – 20 minutes, Cooking time: 15 – 30 minutes; Serve: 6

Ingredients:

- 1 roll of rectangular puff pastry
- 220g of apples
- 50g of sugar
- 100g raisins
- 50g pine nuts
- To taste breadcrumbs
- Cinnamon powder to taste

Direction:

1. Put the raisins in warm water for at least 30 min. Meanwhile, peel the apples, remove the kernel, and cut them into thin slices. Pour the apples into a large bowl and add the dried raisins.
2. Add the cinnamon, sugar, and pine nuts, gently mix the ingredients and let stand.
3. Meanwhile, spread the puff pastry on a work surface with parchment paper. Sprinkle with the breadcrumbs, leaving a 2-3 cm border around. Place the mixture in the center of the dough and close the coating along.
4. Be careful not to tear the dough, close the sides tightly so that the contents do not come out during cooking.
5. Place the liner on the air fryer and Cook over low temperature for about 25 min. When finished cooking, sprinkle the strudel with icing sugar and serve warm sliced.

Nutrition Value (Amount per Serving):

- Calories 411
- Fat 19.38g
- Total Carbohydrate 57.5g
- Sugars 50g
- Protein3.72g
- Cholesterol0mg

Stuffed brioche crown

Preparation time: more than 30 minutes; Cooking time: 30 – 45 minutes; Serve: 8

Ingredients:

- 250g Manitoba flour
- 250g flour 00
- 200 ml of warm milk
- 100 ml of warm water
- 50 ml of olive oil
- 25g baker's yeast
- 1 tbsp sugar
- 1 tsp fine salt
- 250g cooked ham
- 8 slices of emmental
- Poppy seeds
- 1 tbsp of water
- 1 tsp olive oil

Direction:

1. Prepare the brioche crown and let it grow in a lightly floured and closed container with food wrap for about an hour.
2. Once the survey is finished, spread the dough with a rolling pin, forming a narrow rectangle. First place the ham and then the cheese, leaving about 2 cm of free edge around.
3. Roll everything up to get a cylinder. Cut approximately 2 cm slices and place them in the basket covered with baking paper by placing them side by side to form a crown.
4. Let the preparation rise for another hour before cooking. In the end, brush with a mixture of warm water and oil over the entire surface of the crown and sprinkle with poppy seeds.
5. Preheat the air fryer at 180^0C for 5 minutes. Cook for 40 minutes.

Nutrition Value (Amount per Serving):

- Calories 516
- Fat 32g
- Carbohydrates 39g
- Sugars 7g
- Protein 17g
- Cholesterol 0mg

Fried Cream

Preparation time: 10-20 minutes; Cooking time: 15-30 minutes; Serve: 8

Ingredients:

For the cream:

- 500 ml of whole milk
- 3 egg yolks
- 150 g of sugar
- 50 g flour
- 1 envelope Vanilla Sugar

Ingredients for the pie:

- 2 eggs
- Unlimited Breadcrumbs
- 1 tsp oil

Direction:

1. First prepare the custard; once cooked, pour the cream into a dish previously covered with a transparent film and level well. Let cool at room temperature for about 2 hours.
2. Grease the basket and distribute it all over.
3. When the cream is cold, place it on a cutting board and cut it into dice; Pass each piece of cream first in the breadcrumbs, covering the 4 sides well in the beaten egg and then in the pie.
4. Place each part inside the basket. Set the temperature to 150^0C.
5. Cook for 10 to 12 minutes, turning the pieces after 6 to 8 minutes.
6. The doses of this cream are enough to make 2 or even 3 kitchens in a row.

Nutrition Value (Amount per Serving):

- Calories 355
- Fat 18.37g
- Carbohydrates 44.94g
- Sugars 30.36g
- Protein 4.81g
- Cholesterol 45mg

Apple, cream, and hazelnut crumble

Preparation time: 10-20 minutes; Cooking time: 15-30 minutes; Serve: 6

Ingredients:

- 4 golden apples
- 100 ml of water
- 50g cane sugar
- 50g of sugar
- ½ tbsp cinnamon
- 200 ml of fresh cream
- Chopped hazelnuts to taste

Direction:

1. In a bowl, combine the peeled apples, cut into small cubes, cane sugar, sugar, and cinnamon.
2. Pour the apples inside the basket, add the water. Set the air fryer to 180^0C and simmer for 15 minutes depending on the type of apple used and the size of the pieces.
3. At the end, divide the apples in the serving glasses, cover with previously whipped cream and sprinkle with chopped hazelnuts.

Nutrition Value (Amount per Serving):

- Calories 828.8
- Fat 44.8 g
- Carbohydrate 120.6 g
- Sugars 54.2 g
- Protein 4.4 g
- Cholesterol 29.5 mg

Fregolotta (Venetian puff pastry pie) with hazelnuts

Preparation time: 10-20, Cooking time: 15-30, 8 people, Calories: 347

Ingredients:

- 200g of flour
- 150g of sugar
- 100 g melted butter
- 100g hazelnuts
- 1 egg
- ½ sachet of yeast

Direction:

1. Do not finely chop the hazelnuts. In a large bowl, pour all the ingredients (the butter once melted should be cooled before using), mix lightly, without the dough becoming too liquid.
2. Place parchment paper on the bottom of the basket and pour the mixture into it. Spread it evenly.
3. Set the air fryer to 180^0C and simmer for 15 minutes and then turn the cake.
4. Cook for an additional 5 minutes.
5. Let cool and sprinkle the cake with icing sugar.

Nutrition Value (Amount per Serving):

- Calories 465
- Carbohydrates 37g
- Fat 25g
- Sugars 3g
- Protein 20g
- Cholesterol 0mg

Frozen Treats

Cooking time: 15-30 minutes; Serve: 8

Ingredients:

- 14 frozen pieces

Direction:

1. Place the handles, placing them on the parchment paper and place them on the basket.
2. Set the temperature to 150^0C.
3. Cook everything for 25 min.

Nutrition Value (Amount per serving):

- Calories 111
- Fat 20 g
- Carbohydrates 21 g
- Sugars 45g
- Protein 7g
- Cholesterol 0mg

Roscon Of Reyes (Spanish King's Cake)

Preparation time: 10-20 minutes; Cooking time: 30-45 minutes; Serve: 4

Ingredients:

- 2 puff pastries
- 100g almond flour
- 1 egg
- 75g of sugar
- 50g butter
- 1 vial of almond aroma
- 1 porcelain bean

Direction:

First, prepare the filling:

1. In a bowl mix the flour, egg, sugar, butter at room temperature and almond extract.
2. Stretch a puff pastry with the baking paper inside the basket. Prick with a fork and spread the filling well.
3. Place the bean inside, choosing an external position for the cake.
4. Cover with the second roll of puff pastry and weld the edges well. Brush the surface with an egg yolk diluted with milk and decorate with small incisions.
5. Set the temperature to $180^0 C$. Bake the pie for 25 minutes
6. Turn the baking paper half a turn and cook for another 10 minutes.
7. Tradition says that the person who finds the hidden bean becomes the "king" of the day.

Nutrition Value (Amount per Serving):

- Calories 1426
- Fat 10.54g
- Carbohydrates 56.54g
- Sugar 23.51g
- Protein 6.58g
- Cholesterol 29mg

Nut cake

Preparation time: 10-20 minutes, Cooking time: 30-45 minutes; Serve: 10

Ingredients:

- 250 g of walnuts
- 150g Maïzena
- 4 medium eggs
- 200g of butter (room temperature)
- 1 sachet of yeast
- 1 sachet of vanilla sugar
- 200g of sugar

Direction:

1. Chop the nuts with 50 g of sugar. Using a food processor, beat the butter with the remaining sugar until you get a shiny and foamy mixture.
2. Add the eggs one by one, making sure the mixture is still soft, then add the vanilla.
3. Add the chopped nuts with the sugar and then the cornstarch that will sift with the yeast.
4. Butter and flour the basket, then pour the mixture in the center.
5. Set the air fryer at 180°C.
6. Cook for 45 minutes (turn off the lower heating element 40 minutes later). Let cool before serving.

Nutrition Value (Amount per Serving):

- Calories 440
- Fat 20.48g
- Carbohydrate 62.22g
- Sugars 49.65g
- Protein 3.72g
- Cholesterol 53mg

Italian cake

Preparation time: 10-20 minutes; Cooking time: 30-45 minutes; Serve: 8

Ingredients:

- 250g of potato starch
- 150g of flour 00 (flour 55)
- 250g of sugar
- 6 eggs
- 50 g butter
- 1 sachet of yeast
- Powdered sugar

Direction:

1. Melt the butter in a small saucepan and let it cool.
2. Beat the eggs with the fine sugar until you get a light and frothy mixture. Add the flour, starch, sifted yeast, melted butter and mix until a homogeneous mixture is obtained.
3. Butter and flour the basket and pour the preparation into it.
4. Set the temperature to 180^0C and cook the cake for 35 min.
5. Remove the cake from the bowl, let it cool and sprinkle with icing sugar.

Nutrition Value (Amount per Serving):

- Calories 440
- Carbohydrates 40g
- Fat 30g
- Sugars 28g
- Protein 4g
- Cholesterol 65mg

Marble cake

Preparation time: 10-20 minutes; Cooking time: 45-60 minutes; Serve: 10

Ingredients:

- 190g Butter
- 1g bag of vanilla sugar
- 12g baking powder
- 375g Flour
- 22g cocoa powder
- 4g medium eggs
- 225g of sugar
- 165 ml of milk
- Salt (a pinch)

Direction:

1. Put the previously softened butter into small pieces in a bowl with the sugar, mount the ingredients until a white and foamy cream forms.
2. Add the eggs at room temperature, one by one, the salt and beat about 5 minutes until you get a mixture without lumps. Add the flour (except 30 g that will keep aside), the yeast and vanilla sugar sifted alternately with the milk.
3. Mix the ingredients well, then divide them evenly and add the remaining flour in a bowl and the sifted cocoa in another.
4. Butter and flour the basket and first place the transparent mixture divided into three separate parts. Do the same with the dark mixture by filling the remaining gaps between the light mixture.
5. To get the veined effect, rotate a fork from top to bottom through the two colors of the mixture.
6. Set the air fryer to 180^0C and cook for 40 minutes and then turn off the lower resistance.
7. Cook for another 10 min. Control the baking of the cake with the tip of a knife.

Nutrition Value (Amount per Serving):

- Calories 195
- Fat 7.6g
- Carbohydrates 28g
- Sugars 14g
- Protein 3.5g
- Cholesterol 47mg

Genoves Cake

Preparation time: 10-20 minutes; Cooking time: 30-45 minutes; Serve: 10

Ingredients:

- 6 eggs
- 190g of sugar
- 150g of flour 00 (flour 55)
- 75g potato starch
- 2g vanilla sugar

Direction:

1. In a bowl, beat the eggs with the sugar until you get a light and smooth mixture. Add the sifted flour, starch and vanilla sugar and mix with a whisk until a homogeneous mixture is obtained.
2. Butter and flour the basket, then pour the mixture.
3. Set the air fryer to 180^0C and simmer for 35 minutes.

Nutrition Value (Amount per Serving):

- Calories 74
- Fat 1.83g
- Carbohydrate 10.91g
- Sugars 5.08g
- Protein 3.83g
- Cholesterol 74mg

Frozen Sorrentino gnocchi

Cooking time: 0 – 15 minutes; Serve: 2

Ingredients:

- 550 g Sorrentino gnocchi

Direction:

5. Pour the gnocchi in the basket and cook for 13 minutes at 150^0C mixing once halfway through cooking.

Nutrition Value (Amount per Serving):

- Calories 170
- Carbohydrates 30g
- Fat 2g
- Sugars 11g
- Protein 6g
- Cholesterol 5mg

Khachapuri (Georgian bread)

Preparation time: more than 30 minutes; Cooking time: 15 – 30 minutes; Serve: 4

Ingredients:

- 500g of flour
- 450g whole yogurt
- ½ tsp baking soda
- ½ tsp salt
- 150 g ricotta
- 100g provokes smoked
- 150g Greek feta cheese
- 4 tbsp fine parsley

Direction:

1. Prepare the khachapuri dough by mixing all the ingredients until a smooth and homogeneous mixture is obtained. Divide the dough into 8 equal parts.
2. Form 8 balls cover them with a clean cloth. Let them rest in a warm place and away from drafts. After about 1 hour of lifting, start spreading the dough.
3. Meanwhile, prepare the filling by grating provokes smoked and the feta cheese and then mix with the ricotta and parsley.
4. Spread the 8 balls by hand in circles of 10 to 15 cm, fill 4 circles with the previously prepared filling and close with the other 4. Now roll the 4 khachapuri with a roller until you get a diameter of the size of the basket.
5. Grease the bottom of the basket and place 1 khachapuri. Also grease the surface and prick with a fork.
6. Set the air fryer to 180^0C and cook each khachapuri for 15 minutes.

Nutrition Value (Amount per Serving):

- Calories 556
- Fat 33g
- Carbohydrates 37g
- Sugars 3.6g
- Protein 28g
- Cholesterol 181mg

Sweet and Sour Onions

Preparation time: 10-20 minutes, Cooking time: 30-45 minutes; Serve: 8

Ingredients:

- 600g of borretano onions
- 30g butter
- 30g of sugar
- 50g of Modena balsamic vinegar

Direction:

1. First peel and wash the onions.
2. Add the butter and set the air fryer to 160^0C
3. Melt the butter for 2 minutes.
4. Add the sugar and vinegar and cook for another 3 minutes.
5. Then pour the onions and cook them for 30 minutes or to the desired cooking point (this may vary depending on the size of the onions).
6. They can be served as an appetizer or to accompany meat dishes.

Nutrition Value (Amount per Serving):

- Calories 80
- Carbohydrates 17g
- Fat 1g
- Sugars 12g
- Protein 1g
- Cholesterol 0mg

Frozen Paella

Cooking time: 15-30 minutes; Serve: 2

Ingredients:

- 600 g of paella

Direction:

1. Pour the paella in the basket and set the temperature to 150°C.
2. Cook for 15 minutes, mixing once in the middle of cooking.

Nutrition Value (Amount per Serving):

- Calories 315
- Carbohydrates 0g
- Fat 9g
- Protein 0g
- Sugar 0g
- Cholesterol 0mg

Spice Bread

Preparation time: 10 – 20 minutes; Cooking time: 0 – 15 minutes; Serve: 10

Ingredients:

Ingredients for 30 - 35 cookies:

- 350g flour
- 160g of sugar
- 150g of butter
- 1 egg
- 1 pinch of salt
- 150g of honey
- 2 tsp cinnamon
- ¼ tsp nutmeg
- 2 tsp ginger
- ½ tsp of clove (powder)

Direction:

1. Put all the ingredients in a blender (the butter should be cold as soon as it comes out of the fridge).
2. Mix everything until you get a compact and sufficiently elastic mixture. Let it rest in the refrigerator for about 2 hours.
3. Then spread a 4 mm thick puff pastry with the rolling pin. Use templates to cut the dough in several ways.
4. Bake the cookies for 7 minutes at 180^0C, and then rotate the baking paper.
5. Cook for additional 5 minutes, after cooling. Decorate to your liking.

Nutrition Value (Amount per Serving):

- Calories 100
- Fat 0g
- Carbohydrates 21g
- Sugar 6g
- Protein 3g
- Cholesterol 0mg

Rolls

Preparation time: 20 – 30 minutes; Cooking time: 30 – 45 minutes; Serve: 4

Ingredients:

- 20 ml of water
- 350 g flour
- 4 g of sugar
- 6 g of salt
- 10 g fresh yeast

Direction:

1. Put the flour in a large bowl (or on a pastry board), form a hole in the center and pour all the ingredients. Knead everything until you get a ball that you must knead for at least 10 minutes or until it becomes soft and elastic.
2. Cover with a slightly damp cloth and let it grow in a warm room without drafts for at least two hours. The mass should double in volume.
3. When the dough has risen, place it on a floured surface, cut several pieces (according to the size of the bread you want to obtain) and form the bread with your hands.
4. Place the rolls in the basket covered with parchment paper.
5. Set the temperature to 160^0C and simmer for 30 minutes.

Nutrition Value (Amount per Serving):

- Calories 96
- Fat 1.7g
- Carbohydrates 18g
- Sugars 3.1g
- Protein 3.1g
- Cholesterol 0mg

Small Frozen Pizzas

Cooking time: 15-30 minutes; Serve: 8

Ingredients:

- 14 pieces Small frozen pizzas

Direction:

1. Place the small pizzas, place them on the parchment paper, close the lid, place the thermostat in position 3, press the power key of the lower heating element and press the on / off key.
2. Cook everything for 20 minutes at 180^0C.

Nutrition Value (Amount per Serving):

- Calories 350.0
- Fat 16.0 g
- Carbohydrate 38.0 g
- Sugars 3.0 g
- Protein 16.0 g
- Cholesterol 30.0 mg

Small Slippers With Flour

Preparation time: more than 30 minutes, Cooking time: 15 – 30 minutes; Serve: 4

Ingredients:

- 200 ml of water
- 250 g flour
- 250 g Manitoba flour
- 12 g fresh beer yeast
- 10 g of salt
- 5 g of sugar
- 250 g mozzarella
- 150 g of tomato coulis
- Oregano to taste
- Salt to taste

Direction:

1. Pour the flours into a bowl, form a well and then add the other ingredients in the center.
2. Knead by hand until you get soft and flexible dough. Form a ball with this dough and then let it grow in a previously floured bowl.
3. Cover with a clean cloth, let stand in a warm place away from drafts. After about 1 hour of lifting, separate the small slipper by dividing the dough into 8 equal parts to obtain 8 circles.
4. Fill each slipper with the desired ingredients, close the dough to form a crescent and weld the ends well with a fork.
5. Grease the basket and place 4 small turnovers (brush each rotation with a little tomato sauce).
6. Set the air fryer to 150^0C.
7. Cook for another 15 to 20 minutes and then put the other 4 empanadas for cooking.

Nutrition Value (Amount per Serving):

- Calories 455
- Fat 1.2g
- Carbohydrates 95.4g
- Sugars 0.3g
- Protein 12.9g

Peas with Bacon

Preparation time: 10 – 20 minutes, Cooking time: 30 – 45 minutes; Serve: 8

Ingredients:

- 750 g of frozen peas
- 100 g smoked bacon
- 2 shallots
- Salt and pepper to taste
- 200ml broth

Direction:

1. Preheat the air fryer to 160^0C for 5 minutes.
2. Pour the chopped onion, bacon, oil in the basket
3. Brown for 5 min.
4. Add the peas, broth, salt, pepper, and simmer for additional 30 minutes.

Nutrition Value (Amount per Serving):

- Calories 129.6
- Fat 6.0 g
- Carbohydrate 13.6 g
- Sugars 3.3 g
- Protein 6.0 g
- Cholesterol 7.7 mg

Fresh Pizza

Preparation time: 10-20 minutes, Cooking time: 30-45 minutes; Serve: 1

Ingredients:

- 70ml of water
- 125 g flour
- 3g salt
- 7 g fresh yeast
- 100 g of tomato
- 100 g mozzarella
- Oregano to taste

Direction:

1. Pour the flour into a bowl, form a well, and then add the other ingredients in the center.
2. Knead with your hands until you get soft and flexible dough. Form a ball with this dough, and then let it grow in a previously floured bowl.
3. Cover with a clean cloth and let stand at room temperature, away from drafts. After about 1 hour of lifting, start spreading the dough
4. Preheat the air fryer to 150^0C for 5 minutes.
5. Grease the bottom and spread the pizza dough. Cover with tomato coulis. Add a pinch of salt and oregano.
6. After 15 minutes cook add the diced mozzarella
7. Approximately after 10 minutes, turn the pizza half a turn
8. Cook for an additional 7 minutes.

Nutrition Value (Amount per Serving):

- Calories 290
- Carbohydrates 36g
- Fat 11g
- Sugars 0g
- Protein 11g
- Cholesterol 15mg

Frozen Pizza

Cooking time: 15-30 minutes; Serve: 1

Ingredients:

- 1 piece Frozen Pizza

Direction:

1. Cook for 20 minutes at 180^0C turning after 15 minutes.

Nutrition Value (Amount per Serving):

- Calories 576
- Fat 26g
- Carbohydrates 62g
- Sugars 7.7g
- Protein 22g
- Cholesterol 30mg

Poivronnade

Preparation time: 10-20 minutes, Cooking time: 45-60 minutes; Serve: 8

Ingredients:

- 750g Peppers
- 220g onion
- 300 g of tomato puree
- Broth 175g
- Salt and pepper to taste

Direction:

2. First, prepare the ingredients: chop the onion and cut the peppers into strips.
3. Put the onion and oil inside the basket at 150^0C and brown for 5 min.
4. Add peppers, broth, salt, pepper, and simmer for 20 minutes.
5. Then add the tomato and finish cooking for an additional 30 minutes.

Nutrition Value (Amount per Serving):

- Calories 118
- Carbohydrates 5g
- Fat 10g
- Sugars 0g
- Protein 1g
- Cholesterol 0mg

Stuffed Peppers

Preparation time: 10 – 20 minutes, Cooking time: 30 – 45 minutes; Serve: 4

Ingredients:

- 2 Peppers
- 150 g minced meat
- 75 g Sausage
- 40 g French toast
- 1 spoon chopped parsley
- 1 egg
- 50 g grated cheese
- 1 garlic clove
- Salt and pepper to taste
- Butter to taste

Direction:

Prepare the filling:

1. Place all the ingredients, except the peppers, in a food processor (the bread must be soaked in milk to soften it) and mix until a homogeneous and compact compound is obtained.
2. Cut the peppers in half lengthwise, remove the white filaments and seeds.
3. Place the four halves of peppers inside the tray and fill them with the previously prepared mixture. Put in each of them pieces of butter.
4. Set the air fryer to 150^0C and cook for 45 minutes depending on the size of the peppers.

Nutrition Value (Amount per Serving):

- Calories 444
- Fat 24g
- Carbohydrates 30g
- Sugars 8.2g
- Protein 29g
- Cholesterol 121mg

Baked Apples with Cinnamon

Preparation time: 0-10 minutes; Cooking time: 15-30 minutes; Serve: 4

Ingredients:

- 4 golden apples
- 1 roll of rectangular puff pastry
- 100 g apricot jam
- Raisins (sufficient quantity)
- Cinnamon (sufficient quantity)
- Sugar taste

Direction:

1. Peel the apples and remove the core. Unwind the puff pastry and cut it transversely to obtain 4 mini rectangles. Put the apples in the center and fill the hole with jam and some raisins.

2. Sprinkle with cinnamon and sugar (optional) and close with the edges of the puff pastry, pressing well to seal the apple inside. Brush the surface with a little milk to make them color during cooking.

3. Cook for 30 minutes or until desired browning is obtained, at 180^0C.

Nutrition Value (Amount per Serving):

- Calories 173
- Fat 3.2g
- Carbohydrates 39g
- Sugars 32g
- Protein 0.8g
- Cholesterol 7.8mg

Baked Potatoes

Preparation time: 0-10 minutes, Cooking time: more than 60 minutes; Serve: 4

Ingredients:

- 4 whole potatoes (230 g each)
- 4 slices of cheddar cheese
- 20 g butter
- 4 slices of bacon
- Salt to taste
- Pepper to taste

Direction:

1. Wash potatoes well, brushing them gently to remove all traces of dirt without damaging the skin.
2. Cover each potato with oil and cover with a handful of salt (this will make the skin crisp).
3. Place the potatoes in the basket of the pan on parchment paper.
4. Set the air fryer to 160^0C. Simmer for 60 min. (the time varies according to the size of the potatoes used), therefore, it will be useful to verify from time to time that the cooking is perfect.
5. After cooking, cut the potatoes crosswise and dig a little inside. Cover each potato with a piece of butter, a slice of bacon and a slice of cheese.
6. Sprinkle with black pepper and always brown with the thermostat in position 4 for another 3 minutes.

Nutrition Value (Amount per Serving):

- Calories 160.9
- Fat 0.2g
- Carbohydrates 36.6g
- Sugar 2g
- Protein 4.3g
- Cholesterol 160mg

Potatoes with Small Bacon

Preparation time: 10-20 minutes, Cooking time: 30-45 minutes; Serve: 8

Ingredients:

- 1250 g of fresh potatoes(peeled)
- 100 g smoked bacon
- Salt and pepper to taste
- 1 sprig rosemary

Direction:

1. Peel the potatoes and cut them into quarters. Put the potatoes in the water for a few minutes and rinse them well. Drain and clean with a paper towel.
2. Pour the potatoes, rosemary in the basket previously greased, season with salt and pepper.
3. Set the temperature to 150^0C and cook for 15 minutes.
4. Add the bacon and finish cooking, simmer for another 20 minutes.

Nutrition Value (Amount per Serving):

- Calories 180
- Fat 6g
- Carbohydrates 30g
- Sugars 5g
- Protein 3g
- Cholesterol 60mg

Butter and bread pudding (dessert)

Preparation time: 10-20 minutes, Cooking time: 15-30 minutes; Serve: 4

Ingredients:

- 5/6 slices of honey bread
- 30 g butter
- 20 g raisins
- 400 ml of milk
- 4 egg yolks
- 90 g of sugar
- Cinnamon to taste
- 1 vanilla pod

Direction:

1. Remove the crust from the slices of bread and spread the butter on each slice, place them in the container previously buttered.
2. Pour the raisins over the bread. Separately, beat the eggs and sugar with an electric mixer and then add the milk (previously heated with the vanilla pod) until a very homogeneous mixture is obtained.
3. Pour the mixture over the slices of bread, being careful to distribute it evenly. Sprinkle with sugar and cinnamon.
4. Cook at 160^0C for 30 minutes or until desired browning is achieved.
5. Serve hot with whipped cream or jam.

Nutrition Value (Amount per Serving):

- Calories 313
- Fat 15g
- Carbohydrates 36g
- Sugars 13g
- Protein 8.6g
- Cholesterol 98mg

Risotto with Porcini Mushrooms

Preparation time: 0-10 minutes, Cooking time: 15-30 minutes; Serve: 6

Ingredients:

- 320 g of basmati rice
- 200 g of porcini mushrooms
- 1250ml of broth
- 1 clove garlic
- Parsley to taste
- Grated cheese to taste
- Butter to taste

Direction:

1. Grease the basket and add the garlic clove.
2. Set the temperature to 150^0C and brown for 2 minutes.
3. Remove the garlic, add the porcini mushrooms and simmer for another 5 minutes.
4. Add the rice, half the amount of the broth and simmer for another 10 minutes.
5. Pour the rest of the broth and finish cooking for another 13 minutes. Mix 2-3 times with a ladle at the end of cooking.
6. At the end of cooking, add the chopped parsley and mix with butter and grated cheese, serve.

Nutrition Value (Amount per Serving):

- Calories 365.0
- Fat 19.3 g
- Carbohydrate 30.5 g
- Sugars 1.7 g
- Protein 17.5 g
- Cholesterol 50.8 mg

Speck and Cheese Roll

Preparation time: 10 – 20 minutes, Cooking time: 0 – 15 minutes; Serve: 6

Ingredients:

- 1 roll of puff pastry
- 6 speck slices
- 4 slices of provola (spun cheese)

Direction:

1. Unroll the puff pastry and spread the speck slices.
2. Place the cheese slices on the speck and roll the puff pastry until you get a roll. Weld well.
3. Cut the roll into slices and place it inside the mold lined with baking paper.
4. Set the temperature to 180^0C.
5. Cook the rolls for 13 minutes or according to the desired degree of cooking.

Nutrition Value (Amount per Serving):

- Calories 96
- Carbohydrates 8g
- Fat 4g
- Sugars 1g
- Protein 4g
- Cholesterol 6mg

Pesto Rolled and Brie

Preparation time: 10 – 20 minutes, Cooking time: 0 – 15 minutes; Serve: 6

Ingredients:

- 1 roll of puff pastry
- 100 g of brie
- 100 g Genovese pesto

Direction:

1. Unroll the puff pastry and spread the pesto.
2. Cut the cheese into thin slices and cover the pesto. Roll the puff pastry until you get a roll. Weld well.
3. Cut the roll into slices and place it inside the mold lined with baking paper.
4. Set the temperature to 160^0C.
5. Cook the rolls for 13 minutes or according to the desired degree of cooking.

Nutrition Value (Amount per Serving):

- Calories 483
- Sugars 0g
- Carbohydrates 0g
- Protein 35g
- Fat 19g
- Cholesterol 60mg

Santiago's Cake

Preparation time: 10-20 minutes; Cooking time: 30-45 minutes; Serve: 8

Ingredients:

- 250 g of almonds:
- 160 g of sugar
- 6 eggs
- Grated orange rind
- Grated lemon rind
- 5 drops of almond flavor

Direction:

1. In a food processor, chop the almonds until you get flour
2. With an electric mixer, beat the egg yolks with the sugar; add the grated lemon peel, the almond extract and the previously made flour.
3. Separately, beat the egg whites and fold them gently with the rest of the ingredients.
4. Remove the mixing paddle from the tank.
5. Butter and flour the tank and pour the mixture inside.
6. Set the temperature to 180^0C.
7. Bake the cake for 35 minutes.
8. For the final touch, cut a cardboard Santiago cross, place it in the center of the cake and sprinkle with icing sugar. By removing the cross, you will get the design on the cake.

Nutrition Value (Amount per Serving):

- Calories 295.2
- Fat 16.5 g
- Carbohydrate 29.9 g
- Sugars 26.2 g
- Protein 10.1 g
- Cholesterol 142.5 mg

Cream and Pine Nuts Cake

Preparation time: more than 30 minutes, Cooking time: 45-60 minutes; Serve: 10

Ingredients:

- 250 g flour
- 125 g butter
- 110 g of sugar
- 2 eggs (1 whole and egg yolk)
- Salt to taste
- 500ml pastry cream
- 120 g of pine nuts

Direction:

1. Remove the flour, sugar, eggs, butter nuts from the refrigerator and a pinch of salt in the blender.
2. Mix everything until you get a compact and quite flexible mixture. Let it rest in the refrigerator for at least 30 minutes.
3. Butter and flour the basket. Spread the mass of broken dough with a thickness of ¾ cm and place it at the bottom of the basket, carefully cutting the edge.
4. Prick with a fork and spread the custard with a spoon.
5. Finish the cake by covering it completely with pine nuts.
6. Set the air fryer to 180^0C.
7. Cook for 40 minutes and then turn off the lower resistance.
8. Cook another 15 minutes. Cool the cake well before turning it over to turn it off.

Nutrition Value (Amount per Serving):

- Calories 191
- Fat 19g
- Carbohydrates 3.7g
- Sugars 1g
- Protein 3.9g

Ricotta Cake

Preparation time: 10 minutes; Cooking time: 40 minutes; Serve: 10

Ingredients:

- 250 g flour
- 200 g of sugar
- Eggs
- 350 g ricotta
- 120 g melted butter
- 1 sachet of yeast
- 50 g of chocolate chips

Direction:

1. Add ricotta with sugar, add eggs and melted butter. Add the sifted flour with the yeast and finally the chocolate chips.
2. Butter and flour the basket and pour the mixture inside, smearing well.
3. Set the temperature to 180°C and bake the cake for 40 minutes.
4. Let cool and remove it from the basket; sprinkle with icing sugar.

Nutrition Value (Amount per Serving):

- Calories 269
- Fat 9.9g
- Carbohydrates 39g
- Sugars 21g
- Protein 6g
- Cholesterol 64mg

Ricotta Cake and Chocolate Chips

Preparation time: 10-20 minutes, Cooking time: 45-60 minutes; Serve: 10

Ingredients:

For the dough:

- 380g flour
- 165 g of sugar
- 185 g of butter
- 2 eggs
- 1 egg yolk
- 1 pinch of salt

Ingredients for filling:

- 600 g ricotta
- 1 lemon zest
- 100 g of chocolate chips

Direction:

1. Put the flour, sugar, eggs, butter in pieces just outside the refrigerator and a pinch of salt in a blender. Mix everything until you get a compact and sufficiently elastic mixture. Let it rest in the fridge for at least half an hour.

2. Grease and flour the basket. Unroll the mass of broken dough to a thickness of 3-4 mm and cover the bottom and walls. In a bowl, beat the ricotta with the eggs, the sugar, and the lemon zest until you get a smooth and smooth mixture. Finally, add the chocolate chips.

3. Pour everything inside the baking sheet covered with broken dough and slightly bend the edges inwards.

4. Set the temperature to 180^0C.

5. Cook for 40 minutes and then turn off the lowest resistance. Cook for another 10 minutes. Cool well before removing from the baking sheet.

Nutrition Value (Amount per Serving):

- Calories 143.7
- Fat 7.8 g
- Carbohydrate 17.3 g
- Sugars 11.5 g
- Protein 3.0 g
- Cholesterol 28.7 mg

Amandine Pistachio Cake

Preparation time: more than 30 minutes, Cooking time: 30 – 45 minutes; Serve: 8

Ingredients:

For the broken dough:

- 250 g flour
- 110 g of sugar
- 125 g butter
- 2 eggs
- Salt to taste

Direction:

Broken dough:

1. Remove flour, sugar, eggs, butter nuts from the refrigerator and a pinch of salt in the blender.
2. Mix everything until you get a compact and quite flexible mixture. Let it rest in the refrigerator for at least 30 minutes.

Almond cream:

3. Put the chopped almonds, sugar in a blender, and mix everything, then add the flour, eggs and mix well. Separately, cut the pistachios and cut them into large pieces.
4. Butter and flour the bottom of the basket. Unroll the broken dough leaving an edge that may contain almond cream. Prick with a fork and spread the jam.
5. Spread the almond cream and distribute the chopped pine nuts and pistachios.
6. Cook for 45 minutes at 180^0C
7. Let cool and sprinkle with icing sugar.

Nutrition Value (Amount per Serving):

- Calories 242
- Carbohydrates 35g
- Fat 9g
- Sugars 21g
- Protein 3g
- Cholesterol 61mg

Asparagus and Sheep Cheesecake

Preparation time: 10-20 minutes, Cooking time: 15-30 minutes; Serve: 6

Ingredients:

- 250g asparagus
- 6 medium eggs
- ½ white onion
- 30 g grated Roman sheep cheese
- Breadcrumbs to taste
- Salt to taste
- Pepper to taste

Direction:

1. Peel the asparagus tail with a peeler. Cut the tip and boil them in salted water for about 5 to 7 minutes.
2. Cut 3 asparagus, the slightly larger ones in length and set them aside. Cut all others into pieces.
3. Beat the eggs in a bowl with salt and pepper. Add the pecorino and the chopped onion and mix well. Then add the asparagus into pieces and mix gently.
4. Butter the basket and cover with breadcrumbs
5. Pour the egg mixture into the basket. Arrange the asparagus cut lengthwise to beautify the cake.
6. Cook for 15 minutes at 180^0C.

Nutrition Value (Amount per Serving):

- Calories: 548.5
- Fat 41.7 g
- Carbohydrate 22.9 g
- Sugars 4 g
- Protein 21.5 g
- Cholesterol 252.2 mg

Cherry tomato and mozzarella cake

Preparation time: 10 – 20 minutes, Cooking time: 15 – 30 minutes; Serve: 4

Ingredients:

- 1 roll of puff pastry
- ½ yellow pepper
- 100 g mozzarella
- 5 cherry tomatoes
- 2 eggs
- 20 g Parmesan
- 50 ml of milk
- Salt and pepper to taste

Direction:

1. Beat the eggs, milk, Parmesan in a bowl with a little salt and pepper.
2. Unroll the puff pastry (leaving the baking paper) and then prick the bottom with a fork.
3. Arrange the chopped mozzarella, pepper, and sliced tomatoes; pour the prepared preparation.
4. Fold the edges of the dough in and cut the excess baking paper with scissors (keep the ends cut so you can easily rotate and extract the cake).
5. Set the temperature to 160°C and cook another 15 minutes.
6. Turn to 180°C and cook for another 12 minutes (using the baking paper).

Nutrition Value (Amount per Serving):

- Calories 277.8
- Fat 23.5 g
- Carbohydrate 5.1 g
- Sugars 0.6 g
- Protein 13.3 g
- Cholesterol 44.8 mg

Tasty Chicory and Mota Cake

Preparation time: 10-20 minutes, Cooking time: 15-30 minutes; Serve: 6

Ingredients:

- 1 roll of puff pastry
- 200 g of cooked chicory
- 120 g speck in pieces
- 100 ml of fresh cream
- 2 eggs
- 20 g grated cheese:
- 50 ml of milk:
- Salt to taste
- Pepper to taste

Direction:

1. Beat the eggs, cream, grated cheese, and milk in a bowl with a little salt and pepper.
2. Unroll the puff pastry with parchment paper and prick the bottom with the teeth of a fork.
3. Put the speck in pieces and cooked chicory (see recipe "Treviso chicory sauce") in the tank. Add the previously prepared liquid mixture.
4. Fold the edges of the dough and with scissors cut the excess baking paper (keeping some points that will be used to rotate the quiche easily)
5. Cook the cake for 15 minutes at 180° (using parchment paper). Turn and cook for an additional 8 minutes.

Nutrition Value (Amount per Serving):

- Calories 6.7
- Fat 0.1g
- Carbohydrate 1.4g
- Sugars 2g
- Protein 0.5g
- Cholesterol 0.0mg

Frozen Salty Cake

Cooking time: 30-45 minutes; Serve: 6

Ingredients:

- 1 piece of frozen salted cake

Direction:

1. Preheat the air fryer at 160°C for 5 minutes. Place the savory cake in the basket.
2. Cook everything for 45 minutes, turning it to 180°C (using parchment paper) after about 30 minutes.

Nutrition Value (Amount per Serving):

- Calories 250
- Fat 13g
- Carbohydrate 32g
- Sugars 22g
- Protein 2g
- Cholesterol 20mg

Toad in the hole

Preparation time: 10-20 minutes, Cooking time: 30-45 minutes; Serve: 4

Ingredients:

- 8 sausages
- 8 slices of bacon
- 100 g onion
- Thyme to taste

Ingredients for donut dough:

- 130 g flour
- 2 g baking powder
- 1 whole egg
- 1 egg-yolk
- 200 ml of milk
- 100 ml of water
- Salt to taste
- Pepper to taste

Direction:

1. Prepare the donut dough. Beat all the ingredients together until you get a homogeneous mixture without lumps. Cover with the film and let stand for about 10 minutes.
2. Chop the onion and pour it into the tank with the oil; Wrap each sausage with a slice of bacon and place on the onions with a few sprigs of fresh thyme. Pour 100 ml of water.
3. Cook for 15 minutes at 160^0C.
4. Turn the sausages and cook for 10 minutes. At the end of cooking, pour the donut dough over the sausages, turn off the bottom element and close.
5. Cook for 15 to 20 minutes depending on the degree of cooking desired.
6. Serve the toad in the still hot hole with a side sauce

Nutrition Value (Amount per Serving):

- Calories 366
- Fat 23.8g
- Carbohydrates 20.4g
- Fiber 3.4g
- Protein 11.9g
- Cholesterol 160 mg

Asparagus, Cheese and Speck Pie

Preparation time: 10-20 minutes, Cooking time: 30-45 minutes; Serve: 6

Ingredients:

- 150 g of green asparagus
- 150 g of water:
- 1 roll of broken dough
- 100 g of diced mota
- 100 g of Italian cow's milk cheese
- 3 eggs
- 100 ml of milk
- Salt to taste
- Pepper to taste

Direction:

1. Clean the asparagus. Cut them into small pieces and place them in the basket with the water.
2. Set the air fryer to 150^0C.
3. Cook for about 15 minutes.
4. Remove the asparagus from the tank once cooked and wait for them to cool
5. Unroll the broken dough (leaving the baking paper) and then prick the bottom with a fork.
6. Arrange the diced speck and cheese and asparagus, then pour the prepared preparation.
7. Fold the edges of the dough in and cut the excess baking paper with scissors (keep the ends cut so you can easily rotate and extract the cake).
8. Cook another 25 minutes.

Nutrition Value (Amount per Serving):

- Calories 260
- Fat 17g
- Carbohydrates 18g
- Protein 7g

Mushroom, Egg and Mozzarella Cake

Preparation time: 10 minutes; Cooking time: 50 minutes; Serve: 6

Ingredients:

- 2 rolls of puff pastry: 2
- 300 g mushrooms
- 1 onion
- Parsley to taste
- 150 g mozzarella
- 3 eggs

Direction:

1. Clean the mushrooms well and chop them.
2. Spray the basket of the air fryer. Pour the chopped onion in the basket
3. Brown for 2 minutes at 160°C.
4. Add the mushrooms and cook for another 15 minutes. Add (at discretion) salt and pepper, parsley, and finish cooking for another 3 minutes. Meanwhile, prepare hard boiled eggs.
5. In a bowl, mix the mushrooms with the crushed eggs and the chopped mozzarella, salt, and pepper.
6. Unroll the broken dough (leaving the baking paper) and then prick the bottom with a fork.
7. Arrange the egg and mushroom mixture and close with the other dough roll. Weld the edges well.
8. Brush the surface of the dough with egg yolk and prick the steam out.
9. Bake the cake for 30 minutes.

Nutrition Value (Amount per Serving):

- Calories 345.0
- Fat 28.6 g
- Carbohydrate 2.0 g
- Sugars 1.1 g
- Protein 20.4 g
- Cholesterol 464.1 mg

Roasted pears

Preparation time: 5 minutes; Cooking time: 20 minutes; Serve: 2

Ingredients:

4 portions

- 4 pears with rind well washed
- 50 g Raisins
- 2 tbsp jam without sugar
- 1 tsp honey
- 1 pinch cinnamon powder

Direction:

1. Pears are washed, hollowed out by extracting the heart.
2. Separate the pulp
3. Mix the jam chosen with the pulp of pears, honey and raisins and cinnamon
4. Fill the pears with that mixture
5. Place the pears in the fryer
6. In the bowl place a glass of water
7. Cook for 20 minutes at 180^0C
8. Serve them alone or accompanied with a scoop of vanilla ice cream.

Nutrition Value (Amount per Serving):

- Calories 101
- Fat 0.3g
- Carbohydrates 27g
- Fiber 5.5g
- Sugars 17g
- Protein 0.6g

Gluten-Free Yogurt Cake

Preparation time: 10 minutes; Cooking time: 40 minutes; Serve: 2

Ingredients:

- 1 Greek yogurt
- 3 eggs
- 150 g sugar
- 100 g cream
- 50 g sunflower oil
- 50 g butter
- 200 g gluten free flour
- Salt
- 1 on yeast

Direction:

1. Put the eggs, yogurt, and sugar in the basket. Mix well. Add the rest of the ingredients and mix.
2. Put the dough in the sponge cake container, previously brushed with oil. Preheat the fryer and put the mold with the dough for 40 minutes at 170°C.
3. When it cools, unmold, and decorate to taste.

Nutrition Value (Amount per Serving):

- Calories 361.2
- Fat 10.9 g
- Carbohydrate 59.2 g
- Sugars 31.2 g
- Protein 9.6 g
- Cholesterol 53.1 mg

Rösti (Swiss Potatoes)

Preparation time: 10 minutes; Cooking time: 15 minutes; Serve: 4

Ingredients:

- 250 g peeled white potatoes
- 1 tbsp chopped chives
- Freshly ground black pepper
- 1 tbsp olive oil
- 2 tbsp sour cream
- 100 g smoked salmon

Direction:

1. Preheat the air fryer to 180°C. Grate the thick potatoes in a bowl and add three quarters of the scallions and salt and pepper to taste. Mix it well.

2. Grease the pizza tray with olive oil and distribute the potato mixture evenly throughout the pan. Press the grated potatoes against the pan and spread the top of the potato pie with olive oil.

3. Place the pizza tray in the fryer basket and place it in the air fryer. Set the timer to 15 minutes and fry the rösti until it has a pretty brown color on the outside and is soft and well done inside.

4. Cut the rösti into 4 quarters and place each quarter on a plate. Garnish with a tablespoon of sour cream and place the slices of salmon on the plate next to the rösti. Spread the rest of the scallions on sour cream and add a touch of ground pepper.

Nutrition Value (Amount per Serving):

- Calories 123.3
- Fat 6.9 g
- Carbohydrate 7.2 g
- Sugars 0.3 g
- Protein 7.5 g
- Cholesterol 27.4 mg

Thai Fish Cake with Mango Sauce

Preparation time: 20 minutes; Cooking time: 14 minutes; Serve: 4

Ingredients:

- 1 ripe mango
- 1 tsp and a half of red chili paste
- 3 tbsp fresh cilantro or parsley
- 1 lime juice and zest
- 500 g of white fish fillets
- 1 egg
- 1 chopped chive
- 50 g ground coconut

Direction:

1. Peel the mango and cut it into small dice. Mix the mango dice in a bowl with ½ teaspoon of red chili paste, 1 tablespoon of cilantro and the juice and zest of a lime.

2. Beat the fish in the kitchen robot and mix it with 1 egg, 1 teaspoon of salt and the rest of the lime zest, red chili paste and lime juice. Mix everything with the rest of the cilantro, chives and 2 tablespoons of coconut.

3. Place the rest of the coconut on a deep plate. Divide the fish mixture into 12 portions, shape them in round cakes and coat them with the coconut.

4. Place six fish cakes in the basket and place it in the air fryer at 180°C. Set the timer to 7 minutes and fry the cakes until golden brown and ready to drink. Fry in the same way the rest of the fish cakes.

5. Serve with mango sauce.

Nutrition Value (Amount per Serving):

- Calories 361
- Fat 22.8g
- Carbohydrate 13.8g
- Sugars 8.7g
- Protein 25.8g
- Cholesterol 93.9mg

Conclusion

Throughout this book, we have learned a lot about owning and using an air fryer. We can confidently say that the air fryer is one of the best inventions of kitchen appliances.

Healthy food should not be a fad or an impossibility to choose; it should be part of everyone's life. Of course, this does not mean that you must give up enjoying the kitchen; neither of the many dishes that can be prepared healthy. To get it there are certain appliances that can help you and a lot: for example, an air fryer.

In our earlier chapters, you could see that with an air fryer, you will cook different foods in a similar way as a traditional one would. But thanks to its special operation, you can do it without using a single drop of oil. In this way, you can prepare exquisite dishes without added fats and with a considerably lower caloric intake.

Now you know some of the many functions and recipes of an air fryer. We hope that this eBook has helped you discover some interesting features.

Having an air fryer is a great option. You can enjoy a healthier meal and save a good part of the oil expense, all without giving up enjoyable, fried foods

Please enjoy the different recipes that we have listed for you in this cookbook.

Printed in Poland
by Amazon Fulfillment
Poland Sp. z o.o., Wrocław